T0301790

ADVANCES IN
DATA ENVELOPMENT
ANALYSIS

World Scientific–Now Publishers Series in Business

ISSN: 2251-3442

World Scientific – Now Publishers Series in Business: **Vol.8**

ADVANCES IN DATA ENVELOPMENT ANALYSIS

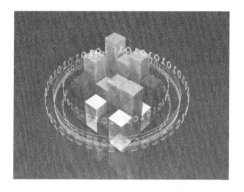

Rolf Färe
Oregon State University, USA

Shawna Grosskopf
Oregon State University, USA

Dimitris Margaritis
University of Auckland, New Zealand

 World Scientific

Published by

World Scientific Publishing Co. Pte. Ltd.
5 Toh Tuck Link, Singapore 596224
USA office: 27 Warren Street, Suite 401-402, Hackensack, NJ 07601
UK office: 57 Shelton Street, Covent Garden, London WC2H 9HE

and

now publishers Inc.
PO Box 1024
Hanover, MA 02339
USA

Library of Congress Cataloging-in-Publication Data
Färe, Rolf, 1942–
    Advances in data envelopment analysis / Rolf Färe, Oregon State University, USA,
Shawna Grosskopf, Oregon State University, USA, Dimitris Margaritis, University of Auckland,
New Zealand.
        pages cm -- (World Scientific-Now Publishers series in business ; vol. 8)
    Includes bibliographical references and index.
    ISBN 978-9814644549 (hardcover) -- ISBN 9814644544 (hardcover)
    1. Data envelopment analysis. 2. Industrial efficiency--Mathematical models. 3. Industrial
productivity--Mathematical models. I. Grosskopf, Shawna. II. Margaritis, Dimitris. III. Title.
    HA31.38.F37 2015
    338.501'51972--dc23
                                                2014048340

British Library Cataloguing-in-Publication Data
A catalogue record for this book is available from the British Library.

In-house Editor: Philly Lim

Typeset by Stallion Press
Email: enquiries@stallionpress.com

Printed in Singapore

Acknowledgements

This volume would not have been written without the support and hospitality of the University of Auckland School of Business, in particular the Department of Finance and Accounting.

Preface

This book synthesizes and disseminates to a wider audience the authors' recent work on DEA (Data Envelopment Analysis) focussing on both theoretical developments and their applications into the measurement of productive efficiency and productivity growth. One of our goals is to guide and prepare the reader to deal with some of the key aspects of DEA often overlooked in empirical work such as diagnostic tests to determine whether the data conform with technology which in turn is important in identifying technical change, or finding which types of DEA models allow data transformations, including dealing with ordinal data. Another goal is to familiarize the reader with recent advances in DEA as they apply to the modelling of time substitution, i.e. the problem of how to allocate resources over time.

We start with an overview of the different formulations of the DEA technology that we use in this monograph. This is followed by a discussion of properties satisfied by the DEA technology. We also provide a direct link to the early work using Activity Analysis Models and linear programming associated with Koopmans (1951), Dorfman, Samuelson and Solow (1958) introducing a technology matrix, and show how this is linked to the DEA framework.

Chapter 2 focuses on what we can learn about technology directly from the data. We begin with what we call 'diagnostic tests' to determine whether the sample data satisfy the Kemeny, Morgenstern and Thompson (1956) conditions on inputs and outputs introduced in Chapter 1 which are essential for establishing that the technology set is closed and the output set is bounded. We also provide a diagnostic to determine whether undesirable outputs such as pollution are jointly produced with desirable outputs. In the DEA world technical change is usually estimated using a Malmquist productivity change index. We use the analysis of the data matrices to identify the DMU which is most efficient in changing their technology over time, and hence identifying technical change. After our diagnostics we take up data transformations and DEA. In particular we investigate 'allowable' changes in unit of measurement of data, including affine changes.

In Chapter 3 we take a different look at the intensity variables which are typically used to construct the technology and identify peer DMUs. Following work in financial economics, we use the duals of these variables to estimate the 'value' of a DMU. First, we show how the duality between input quantities and input prices was developed by Shephard (1953). We then consider the more general case including both inputs and outputs with an emphasis on the DEA technology via the introduction of the adjoint transformation associated with this technology. We illustrate the use of the adjoint transformation of the technology matrix by revisiting the Diet Problem to show how this classical linear programming problem is related to DEA. We show that the dual to the diet problem is dual to revenue or profit maximization problem (depending on the formulation) in DEA. And we build on the idea of pricing securities, as in Magill and Quinzii (1996), to lay out the theoretical foundations for pricing DMUs. The idea consists of studying the adjoint transformation associated with the DEA technology, specifically using the intensity variables to map the DEA technology matrix into input-output space.

In Chapter 4 we undertake an in-depth study of directional distance functions and how they apply to DEA. We begin the chapter with a discussion of the directional vectors and how they influence the DEA scores for inefficient DMUs. We next consider the role of the direction vectors when the goal is to aggregate across DMUs. Here we show that aggregation is facilitated when the DMUs are given the same direction vector, in particular the unit direction. The concluding section addresses the choice of direction in general, and how to endogenize that choice in particular. This leads us to a discussion of directional distance functions and their indication properties, i.e., the subsets of the technology to which the DMUs under evaluation are projected. We also show how the endogenization of the directions is related to slack-based directional distance functions.

Chapter 5 addresses a single DEA topic, time substitution. This topic is the study of how to allocate resources in time, with the two options (i) determine when to apply inputs and (ii) how long, i.e., in how many periods should inputs be used. These options allow the decision maker to determine when to start production and for how long to produce. After an introductory theoretical presentation we devote the rest of the chapter to an empirical application examining the Pact for Stability and Growth adopted by the countries comprising the single currency Euro zone.

In Chapter 6 we discuss the limitations of two DEA models. The first is the DEA specification with a non-Archimedean infinitesimal and the second is the 'super-efficiency' model. The first of these was introduced to address Charnes, Cooper and Rhodes' (1978) concern that the piecewise linear construction of technology in DEA may yield vertical and horizontal extensions. The super-efficiency model was introduced by Andersen and Petersen (1993) to provide a means to 'break ties', i.e., to allow for ranking the DMUs in a sample which are technically efficient. For these two problems we provide an example which demonstrates the limitations of these 'fixes.' In the case of the non-Archimedian, we show that a slight change in the choice of the approximation for the non-Archimedean can result in changes in the rankings of DMUs. For the super-efficiency model we provide an example showing that this approach may fail to break ties.

Contents

Chapter 1

Introduction

The purpose of our first chapter is to review the basic building blocks used as the foundation for the rest of this monograph. These will be familiar to the Data Envelopment Analysis (DEA) audience, although our notation and orientation toward axiomatic production theory may be less familiar.

We begin with the DEA technology constructed from data generated by activities of DMUs (Decision Making Units). To transform sample data points into a technology set, intensity variables, familiar from Activity Analysis are introduced. These allow us to form the basic DEA technology satisfying strong disposability of inputs and outputs as well as constant returns to scale (CRS). We start with three variations of the technology: (i) the (input–output) technology set, (ii) the output sets, and (iii) the input sets. These three equivalent representations allow us to highlight or focus on various features of production such as returns to scale, or substitution among outputs or inputs.

To provide a more direct link to the early work using Activity Analysis Models and linear programming associated with Koopmans (1951), Dorfman, Samuelson and Solow (1958), we also introduce a technology matrix M, and show how this is linked to the DEA framework.

In Section 2 we discuss properties satisfied by the DEA technology. We also show how the conditions proposed by Kemeny, Morgenstern and Thompson (1956) are essential to prove some fundamental economic and mathematical properties: (i) no free lunch, (ii) scarcity, and (iii) closedness.

An appendix of proofs concludes the chapter.

1.1   The DEA Technology and Its Representation

In this section we introduce the different formulations of the DEA technology we use in this monograph. In terms of notation we assume that there are $x = (x_1, \ldots, x_N) \in \Re_+^N$ inputs used to produce $y = (y_1, \ldots, y_M) \in \Re_+^M$ outputs. Each input and output is a nonnegative real number; thus we are assuming that inputs and outputs are divisible.[1] This is a simplifying assumption which may be modified if required. For example, it is difficult to think of producing π number of cars.

Our three basic specifications of the technology are

- $T = \{(x, y) : x \text{ can produce } y\}$ **Technology Set**
- $P(x) = \{y : x \text{ can produce } y\}$ **Output Set**
- $L(y) = \{x : x \text{ can produce } y\}$ **Input Set**

The equivalence relationship among the sets may be summarized as **Lemma 1:1** $(x, y) \in T \Leftrightarrow y \in P(x) \Leftrightarrow x \in L(y)$.[2]

To provide some intuition concerning the relationships among these three representations of technology assume that we have one input employed to produce one output. Our three sets are illustrated in Figure 1.1.

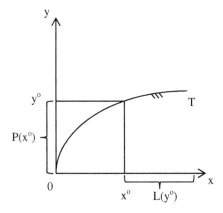

Fig. 1.1.   Illustration of technology sets.

---

[1]For a discussion of production theory with indivisibilities, see Bobzin (1998).

[2]We note that this equivalence holds 'in general'; it does not require any particular structure on the different sets. Berge (1963) discusses inverses of correspondences, i.e., set-valued mappings such as $P(x)$ and $L(y)$.

In the figure, the technology set T consists of the input output vectors on and below the curve. The output set for a given input x^o is the segment of the output axis including y^o and southward to the origin, labeled $P(x^o)$ in the figure. The corresponding input set for output level y^o is the x-axis beginning at x^o and extending eastward, labeled $L(y^o)$ in the figure. Generalizing to multiple inputs and outputs would yield images of our input and output sets as more familiar upper level sets and production possibility sets, respectively.

In order to formulate the DEA or Activity Analysis models of these three representations of technology we assume that there are $k = 1, \ldots, K$ observations or DMUs, which can be farms, firms, etc., each represented by an input–output vector

$$(x_{k1}, \ldots, x_{kN}, y_{k1}, \ldots, y_{kM})'. \tag{1.1}$$

Taking all K DMUs together, they form a set of column vectors:

$$\begin{pmatrix} x_{11} & \cdots & x_{k1} & \cdots & x_{K1} \\ \vdots & \ddots & \vdots & \ddots & \vdots \\ x_{1N} & \cdots & x_{kN} & \cdots & x_{KN} \\ y_{11} & \cdots & y_{k1} & \ddots & y_{K1} \\ \vdots & \ddots & \vdots & \ddots & \vdots \\ y_{1M} & \cdots & y_{kM} & \cdots & y_{KM} \end{pmatrix}$$

where each column represents the data for one DMU. To transform this data matrix into the DEA technology matrices, nonnegative intensity variables are introduced, $z_k, k = 1, \ldots, K$, i.e., one for each DMU. Together with the data matrix the DEA model follows as

$$z_1 \begin{pmatrix} x_{11} \\ \vdots \\ x_{1N} \\ y_{11} \\ \vdots \\ y_{1M} \end{pmatrix} + \cdots + z_k \begin{pmatrix} x_{k1} \\ \vdots \\ x_{kN} \\ y_{k1} \\ \vdots \\ y_{kM} \end{pmatrix} + \cdots + z_K \begin{pmatrix} x_{K1} \\ \vdots \\ x_{KN} \\ y_{K1} \\ \vdots \\ y_{KM} \end{pmatrix}.$$

This may be rewritten as a DEA technology set

$$T = \left\{ (x, y) : \sum_{k=1}^{K} z_k x_{kn} \leqq x_n, \quad n = 1, \ldots, N \right.$$ (1.2)

$$\sum_{k=1}^{K} z_k y_{km} \geqq y_m, \quad m = 1, \ldots, M$$

$$\left. z_k \geqq 0, \quad k = 1, \ldots, K \right\}.$$

A corresponding output set is

$$P(x^o) = \left\{ (y) : \sum_{k=1}^{K} z_k x_{kn} \leqq x_n^o, \quad n = 1, \ldots, N \right.$$ (1.3)

$$\sum_{k=1}^{K} z_k y_{km} \geqq y_m, \quad m = 1, \ldots, M$$

$$\left. z_k \geqq 0, \quad k = 1, \ldots, K \right\}$$

with an input set

$$L(y^o) = \left\{ x : \sum_{k=1}^{K} z_k x_{kn} \leqq x_n, \quad n = 1, \ldots, N \right.$$ (1.4)

$$\sum_{k=1}^{K} z_k y_{km} \geqq y_m^o, \quad m = 1, \ldots, M$$

$$\left. z_k \geqq 0, \quad k = 1, \ldots, K \right\}.$$

Note that y^o is given for the input set and x^o is given for the output set and neither is given for the technology set.

Later in this manuscript we will make use of the technology matrix consisting of the sample DMUs' data, which we denote as M. In this matrix we take input quantities as nonpositive values. This allows us to specify the sets above without reversing inequalities for inputs and outputs as we did above,

$$M = \begin{pmatrix} -x_{11} & \cdots & -x_{k1} & \cdots & -x_{K1} \\ \vdots & \ddots & \vdots & \ddots & \vdots \\ -x_{1N} & \cdots & -x_{kN} & \cdots & -x_{KN} \\ y_{11} & \cdots & y_{k1} & \ddots & y_{K1} \\ \vdots & \ddots & \vdots & \ddots & \vdots \\ y_{1M} & \cdots & y_{kM} & \cdots & y_{KM} \end{pmatrix}.$$

The technology set T and the technology matrix M are related by[3]

$$Mz \geqq (-x, y)' = T, \quad z \in \Re_+^K. \tag{1.5}$$

In the next section we study the axiomatic properties of the DEA technology. This is despite the quote from a referee report which we received: '...CCR do not assume constant returns to scale.'[4]

1.2 (Axiomatic) Properties of the DEA Model

In his original work on Activity Analysis, von Neumann (1937,1945) assumed that inputs and outputs were strictly positive for each observation (DMU). The same assumption was made by Charnes, Cooper and Rhodes (1978). This assumption was relaxed by Kemeny, Morgenstern and Thompson (1956) to the following conditions on the data:

(i) $\displaystyle\sum_{m=1}^{M} y_{km} > 0, \quad k = 1, \ldots, K,$ (ii) $\displaystyle\sum_{k=1}^{K} y_{km} > 0, \quad m = 1, \ldots, M,$

(iii) $\displaystyle\sum_{n=1}^{N} x_{kn} > 0, \quad k = 1, \ldots, K,$ (iv) $\displaystyle\sum_{k=1}^{K} x_{kn} > 0, \quad n = 1, \ldots, N.$

$$\tag{1.6}$$

---

[3]This formulation follows Koopmans (1951) and Dorfman, Samuelson and Solow (1958).
[4]Referee report on Byrnes, Färe and Grosskopf (1984); CCR is Charnes Cooper and Rhodes (1978).

The condition (i) states that each DMU produces at least one type of output, (ii) states that each output is produced by at least one DMU. Similarly the last two conditions require that each DMU use at least one input and each input is employed by at least one DMU. These four conditions allow us to have data in the technology matrix with some zeros as long as we have at least one nonzero element in each column and row. These conditions are easy to verify from simple inspection of the data. This means that our technology matrix may be of the form

$$
\begin{pmatrix}
-1 & 0 \\
0 & -1 \\
1 & 1
\end{pmatrix}
$$

where the columns are associated with the two DMUs, and the first two rows refer to inputs and the last row to the single output. The DEA technology T derived from these data may be written as

$$
T = \{(x, y) : z_1 \cdot 1 + z_2 \cdot 0 \leqq x_1 \tag{1.7}
$$
$$
z_1 \cdot 0 + z_2 \cdot 1 \leqq x_2
$$
$$
z_1 \cdot 1 + z_2 \cdot 1 \geqq y
$$
$$
z_1, z_2 \geqq 0\}.
$$

This is more interesting in terms of the input set

$$
L(y) = \{x : z_1 \cdot 1 + z_2 \cdot 0 \leqq x_1 \tag{1.8}
$$
$$
z_1 \cdot 0 + z_2 \cdot 1 \leqq x_2
$$
$$
z_1 \cdot 1 + z_2 \cdot 1 \geqq y
$$
$$
z_1, z_2 \geqq 0\},
$$

which is illustrated in Figure 1.2.

Next we turn to the properties satisfied by the DEA model, beginning with two that rely on the Kemeny, Morgenstern and Thompson (1956) conditions.

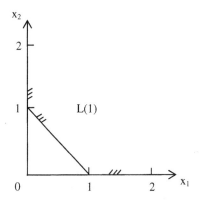

Fig. 1.2. Input set for data satisfying Kemeny, Morgenstern and Thompson (1956).

P.1 $x = 0 \Rightarrow P(x) = \{0\}$, **no free lunch**

Sketch of proof: Let $x = 0$ and consider the following input constraints

$$z_1 x_{11} + \cdots + z_K x_{K1} \leqq 0 \qquad (1.9)$$

$$\vdots \qquad\qquad \vdots$$

$$z_1 x_{1n} + \cdots + z_K x_{Kn} \leqq 0$$

$$\vdots \qquad\qquad \vdots$$

$$z_1 x_{1N} + \cdots + z_K x_{KN} \leqq 0$$

Condition (iii) from Kemeny, Morgenstern and Thompson (1956) says that each DMU has at least one positive x_{kn}. Thus each z_k is multiplied by at least one positive coefficient x_{kn}, hence since $z_k \geqq 0$, and the right hand side is 0, $z_k = 0$ for each k. Thus looking at the output constraints the only possible output is 0, proving **P.1**.

P.2 $P(x)$ is bounded for all x, **scarcity**

This condition tells us that finite inputs can only produce finite outputs. The proof is in the appendix to this chapter.

P.3 T is a closed set.

T is closed if $(x^l, y^l) \rightarrow (x^o, y^o)$ with $(x^l, y^l) \in T$ for all l, then $(x^o, y^o) \in T$.

Note that T closed implies that $P(x)$ and $L(y)$ are closed. This follows by taking $x^l = x^o$ and $y^l = x^o$, respectively, since

$$y^l \in P(x^o) \quad \text{for all } l, (y^l, x^o) \to (y^o, x^o), \qquad (1.10)$$

and $(y^o, x^o) \in T \to y^o \in P(x^o)$.

$P(x)$ bounded (**P.2**) and closed (**P.3**) makes $P(x)$ a compact set.

The same logic applies to $L(y)$ closed. The proof of T closed is found in the appendix to this chapter.

P.4 $y \in P(x), y' \leq y \Rightarrow y' \in P(x)$, **strong disposability of outputs**

This property follows from the inequalities of the output constraints.

P.5 $x \in L(y), x' \geq x \Rightarrow x' \in L(y)$, **strong disposability of inputs**

This follows from the inequalities on the input constraints.

P.6 T is a convex set.

Note that if T is convex, then $P(x)$ and $L(y)$ are also convex.[5] By convexity of T, we mean

$$(x, y), (x', y') \in T, \quad 0 \leq \lambda \leq 1 \Rightarrow \lambda(x, y) + (1 - \lambda)(x', y') \in T \quad (1.11)$$

---

[5]The converse is not true, as the following example shows: Figure: $P(x)$ and $L(y)$ convex does not imply that T is convex.

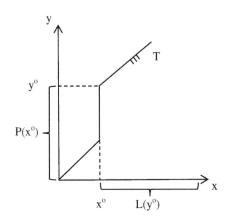

As we did above we can extend this to $L(y)$, by setting $y = y'$, then we have

$$x, x' \in L(y) \Rightarrow \lambda x + (1 - \lambda)x' \in L(y). \qquad (1.12)$$

The same type of argument may be applied to show that if T is convex, then $P(x)$ is convex. The formal proof of the convexity of T is in the appendix to this chapter.

P.7 $\lambda T = T, \lambda > 0$, **constant returns to scale**

Note that $\lambda T = T \Leftrightarrow P(\lambda x) = \lambda P(x) \Leftrightarrow L(\theta y) = \theta L(y), \theta > 0$. We begin by proving that $\lambda T = T \Rightarrow P(\lambda x) = \lambda P(x)$:

Let $(\lambda x, \lambda y) \in T \Leftrightarrow \lambda y \in P(\lambda x) \Rightarrow (x, y) \in T \Leftrightarrow y \in P(x)$. Then multiply by λ and we have $\lambda y \in \lambda P(x) \Rightarrow P(\lambda x) \subseteq \lambda P(x)$.

Conversely let $(x, y) \in T \Leftrightarrow y \in P(x)$ Then by CRS this implies that $(\lambda x, \lambda y) \in T \Leftrightarrow \lambda y \in P(\lambda x) \Rightarrow y \in 1/\lambda P(x) \Rightarrow \lambda P(x) \subseteq P(\lambda x)$. Thus $P(\lambda x) \subseteq \lambda P(x) \subseteq P(\lambda x)$, thus $P(\lambda x) = \lambda P(x)$.

We can also show that the DEA technology satisfies CRS, i.e., $P(\lambda x^o) = \lambda P(x^o)$:

$$P(\lambda x^o) = \left\{ y : \sum_{k=1}^{K} z_k x_{kn} \leqq x_n^o \lambda, \quad n = 1, \dots, N \right. \qquad (1.13)$$

$$\sum_{k=1}^{K} z_k y_{km} \geqq y_m, \quad m = 1, \dots, M$$

$$\left. z_k \geqq 0, \quad k = 1, \dots, K \right\}$$

$$= \lambda \left\{ y/\lambda : \sum_{k=1}^{K} z_k/\lambda x_{kn} \leqq x_n^o, \quad n = 1, \dots, N \right. \qquad (1.14)$$

$$\sum_{k=1}^{K} z_k/\lambda y_{km} \geqq y_m/\lambda, \quad m = 1, \dots, M$$

$$\left. z_k/\lambda \geqq 0, \quad k = 1, \dots, K \right\}.$$

The desired result follows from defining $\hat{y}_m = y_m/\lambda, m = 1, \ldots, M$ and $\hat{z}_k = z_k/\lambda, k = 1, \ldots, K$.

We say that technology satisfies nonincreasing returns to scale (NIRS) if

$$z_k \geqq 0, \quad k = 1, \ldots, K \quad \text{and} \quad \sum_{k=1}^{K} z_k \leqq 1, \tag{1.15}$$

and we say that it exhibits variable returns to scale (VRS) if

$$z_k \geqq 0, \quad k = 1, \ldots, K \quad \text{and} \quad \sum_{k=1}^{K} z_k = 1. \tag{1.16}$$

The three scale models are illustrated in Figure 1.3 with two DMUs.

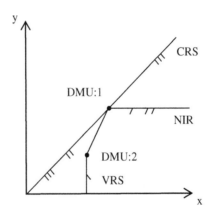

Fig. 1.3.   Illustration of returns to scale.

The three models are nested in the following sense

$$T(\text{CRS}) \supseteq T(\text{NIRS}) \supseteq T(\text{VRS}). \tag{1.17}$$

Returning to disposability properties, we note that circumstances may arise in which strong disposability of inputs or outputs may not be appropriate. For example, if the goal is to measure congestion, that won't be possible if strong disposability is assumed and imposed. In the case of outputs, joint production of good and bad outputs such as electric power and SO_2, imposing strong disposability implies that the bad outputs may be costlessly disposed.

Thus, following Shephard (1974), we introduce an alternative disposability property, namely weak disposability of inputs and outputs. We say that outputs are weakly disposable if

P.4.W $y \in P(x)$ and $0 \leqq \theta \leqq 1$ imply $\theta y \in P(x)$.

And we say that inputs are weakly disposable if

P.5.W $x \in L(y)$ and $\lambda \geqq 1$ imply $\lambda x \in L(y)$.

Note that although strong disposability implies weak disposability, the converse is not true as seen from the next two figures.

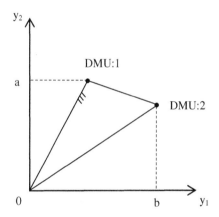

Fig. 1.4.   Strong and weak disposability of outputs.

Figure 1.4 illustrates output disposablity. The weakly disposable output set is bounded by 0-DMU1-DMU2-0, while the strongly disposable output set is bounded by 0-a-DMU1-DMU2-b-0. The two sets would be equal if there were DMUs at points a and b.

To illustrate weak input disposability assume two inputs are used to produce output, see Figure 1.5.

The weakly disposable input set is bounded by the line segments connecting DMU1 and DMU2, as well as the radial expansions from the DMUs input bundles. Strong disposability — which is generated by the inequalities on the input constraints — allows for vertical and horizontal extensions from the DMU input bundles, generating the broken lines in the figure. Again if the DMUs are on the boundary of $\Re_{+}^{2}$, the two sets coincide.

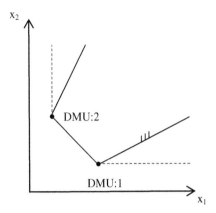

Fig. 1.5.   Strong and weak disposability of inputs.

In the case of CRS and NIRS, the specification of the DEA technology under weak rather than strong disposability of *outputs*, requires only that the inequalities in the output constraints be changed to strict equalities, which we write out for the CRS case below.

$$P(x|W) = \left\{ y : \sum_{k=1}^{K} z_k x_{kn} \leqq x_n, \quad n = 1, \ldots, N \right. \tag{1.18}$$

$$\sum_{k=1}^{K} z_k y_{km} = y_m, \quad m = 1, \ldots, M$$

$$\left. z_k \geqq 0, \quad k = 1, \ldots, K \right\}.$$

To prove that $P(x|W)$ satisfies weak disposability of outputs let $y \in P(x|W)$, then there exist $z_k^o \geqq 0, k = 1, \ldots, K$ such that

$$\sum_{k=1}^{K} z_k^o x_{kn} \leqq x_n, \quad n = 1, \ldots, N$$

$$\sum_{k=1}^{K} z_k^o y_{km} = y_m, \quad m = 1, \ldots, M. \tag{1.19}$$

Multiply both expressions by $\theta, 0 \leqq \theta \leqq 1$:

$$\theta \sum_{k=1}^{K} z_k^o x_{kn} \leqq \theta x_n, \quad n = 1, \ldots, N$$

$$\theta \sum_{k=1}^{K} z_k^o y_{km} = \theta y_m, \quad m = 1, \ldots, M. \tag{1.20}$$

Define $\hat{z}_k = \theta z_k^o$, then $\hat{z}_k \geqq 0, k = 1, \ldots K$, thus

$$\sum_{k=1}^{K} \hat{z}_k x_{kn} \leqq \theta x_n \leqq x_n, \quad n = 1, \ldots, N$$

$$\sum_{k=1}^{K} \hat{z}_k y_{km} = \theta y_m, \quad m = 1, \ldots, M \tag{1.21}$$

showing that $\theta y \in P(x|W)$.

In the case of VRS a scaling factor must be introduced,[6] so the output set takes the form

$$P(x|W|V) = \left\{ y : \sum_{k=1}^{K} z_k x_{kn} \leqq x_n, \qquad n = 1, \ldots, N \right.$$

$$\mu \sum_{k=1}^{K} z_k y_{km} = y_m, \qquad m = 1, \ldots, M$$

$$z_k \geqq 0, \ k = 1, \ldots, K, \ \sum_{k=1}^{K} z_k = 1$$

$$\left. 0 \leq \mu \leq 1 \right\}.$$

This model was extended by Kuosmanen (2005) to use separate scaling factors for each output, thus the output constraint becomes

$$\mu_m \sum_{k=1}^{K} z_k y_{km} = y_m, \quad 0 \leqq \mu \leqq 1, \quad m = 1, \ldots, M. \tag{1.22}$$

---

[6]Shephard (1974).

To accommodate weak disposability of inputs we again have two cases:

1. CRS and NIRS
2. VRS.

For CRS and NIRS we impose weak disposability of inputs by changing the inequalities in the input constraints to strict equalities

$$\sum_{k=1}^{K} z_k x_{kn} = x_n, \quad n = 1, \ldots, N. \tag{1.23}$$

And in the case of VRS we add a scaling factor $\delta \geqq 1$ to the above constraint as follows

$$\delta \sum_{k=1}^{K} z_k x_{kn} = x_n, \quad n = 1, \ldots, N. \tag{1.24}$$

We note that as with the output case, one could specify individual input scaling factors $\delta_n, n = 1, \ldots, N, \delta \geqq 1$.

1.3 Appendix

Proposition A.1 The DEA output set $P(x)$ is bounded.

Proof:[7] Let $x^o \in \Re_+^N$ and consider the set of feasible intensity variables

$$\left\{ (z_1, \ldots, z_K) : \sum_{k=1}^{K} z_k x_{kn} \leqq x_n^o, \quad n = 1, \ldots, N \right. \tag{1.25}$$

$$\left. z_k \geqq 0, \quad k = 1, \ldots, K \right\}.$$

By the Kemeny, Morgenstern and Thompson (1956) conditions (iii) and (iv) this set is bounded, i.e., each $z_k \leqq z_k^o, k = 1, \ldots, K$ for some firm z_k^o. Thus each y_m is bounded above, showing that $P(x)$ is bounded.

Q.E.D.

---

[7]This proof and the proofs of other conditions are also found in Shephard (1970).

Proposition A.2 The DEA technology is a closed set.

Proof: Let $(x^l, y^l) \to (x^o, y^o)$ with $(x^l, y^l) \in T$ for all l, thus $y^l \in P(x^l)$ for all l. We need to show that $y^o \in P(x^o)$ since then $(x^o, y^o) \in T$. $y^l \in P(x^l)$ implies that there is a sequence $z^l = (z_1^l, \ldots, z_K^l)$ such that

$$\sum_{k=1}^{K} z_k^l x_{kl} \leqq x_l^k \quad \text{for all inputs}$$

$$\sum_{k=1}^{K} z_k^l y_{km} \geqq y_m^l \quad \text{for all outputs.}$$

Since $x^l \to x^o$, there is an $\overline{x} \geq x^l$ for all l, thus by conditions (iii) and (iv) the set

$$z = \left\{ (z_1, \ldots, z_K) : \sum_{k=1}^{K} z_k x_{kn} \leqq \overline{x}_n, \quad n = 1, \ldots, N \right.$$

$$\left. z_k \geqq 0, \quad k = 1, \ldots, K \right\} \quad (1.26)$$

is compact, and there is a subsequence $z^{n_l} \to z^o$. Hence since $\sum_{k=1}^{K} z_k x_{kn}, n = 1, \ldots, N$ and $\sum_{k=1}^{K} z_k y_{km}$ are continuous, it follows that

$$\sum_{k=1}^{K} z_k^l x_{kn} \leqq x_n^k \quad \text{for all inputs}$$

$$\sum_{k=1}^{K} z_k^l y_{km} \geqq y_m^k \quad \text{for all outputs}$$

converge so

$$\sum_{k=1}^{K} z_k^o x_{kn} \leqq x_n^o, \quad n = 1, \ldots, N$$

$$\sum_{k=1}^{K} z_k^o y_{km} \geqq y_m^o, \quad m = 1, \ldots, M.$$

And therefore $y^o \in P(x^o)$ or equivalently $(x^o, y^o) \in T$. **Q.E.D.**

Proposition A.3 The DEA technology T is a convex set.

Proof: Let (x, y) and $(x', y') \in T$. Then there are vectors z and z' such that

$$zX \leqq x \quad y \leqq zY$$
$$z'X \leqq x' \quad y' \leqq z'Y$$

where X denotes the input 'submatrix' of **M** and Y is the output submatrix of **M**.

Then

$$(\lambda z + (1 - \lambda)z')X \leqq \lambda x + (1 - \lambda)x'$$

and

$$\lambda y + (1 - \lambda)y' \leqq (\lambda z + (1 - \lambda)z')Y$$

where $0 \leqq \lambda \leqq 1$.

Since

$$(\lambda z + (1 - \lambda)z') \geqq 0,$$
$$(\lambda x + (1 - \lambda)x', \lambda y + (1 - \lambda)y') \in T. \quad \textbf{Q.E.D.}$$

Chapter 2

Looking at the Data in DEA

This chapter focuses on what we can learn about technology directly from the data, before we introduce the structure imposed by the assumptions set out in the previous chapter. We also address issues of allowable transformations of the raw data. Allowable in the sense that the resulting efficiency scores are invariant to those transformations for two specific DEA models: the Charnes, Cooper and Rhodes (1978) or von Neumann (1938, 1945) models, and the variable returns to scale directional distance function model.

We begin with what we call 'diagnostic tests' to determine whether the sample data satisfy the Kemeny, Morgenstern and Thompson (1956) conditions introduced in the previous chapter. These conditions on inputs and outputs provide minimal conditions which are essential for proving that the technology set is closed and the output set is bounded. We also provide a diagnostic to determine whether specific outputs are 'null-joint' with others, e.g., whether undesirable outputs are jointly produced with desirable outputs.

We devote the next section to the analysis of our data with respect to identifying technical change.

After our diagnostics we take up data transformations and DEA. In particular we investigate 'allowable' changes in unit of measurement of data, including affine changes. An appendix with details on distance functions concludes this chapter.

2.1   Data Diagnostics

The Kemeny, Morgenstern and Thompson (1956) conditions on allowable data for inputs and outputs in DEA were introduced in Chapter 1. Some of these conditions were used to prove properties on the DEA technology. Here we discuss those properties with respect to: (i) whether the data satisfy them, and (ii) how to interpret them.

We also provide a diagnostic to determine whether a particular data set satisfies what we call null jointness, which obtains when some outputs are produced as byproducts of others. A familiar example would be the joint production of pollution with a marketable output. This is the example referred to by Baumgärtner *et al.* (2001, p. 365) when they claim: '...the production of wanted goods gives rise to additional unwanted goods...'

Returning to the Kemeny, Morgenstern and Thompson (1956) conditions, recall

$$(i) \sum_{k=1}^{K} y_{km} > 0, \ m = 1, \ldots, M, \quad (ii) \sum_{m=1}^{M} y_{km} > 0, \ k = 1, \ldots, K,$$

$$(iii) \sum_{k=1}^{K} x_{kn} > 0, \ n = 1, \ldots, N, \quad (iv) \sum_{n=1}^{N} x_{kn} > 0, \ k = 1, \ldots, K.$$

$$(2.1)$$

To illustrate, assume that we have two DMUs (K = 2) which employ two inputs (N = 2) to produce two outputs (M = 2). We decompose the technology matrix into an input matrix X and an output matrix Y, both consisting of nonnegative numbers, i.e.,

$$X = \begin{pmatrix} x_{11} & x_{21} \\ x_{12} & x_{22} \end{pmatrix}, \quad Y = \begin{pmatrix} y_{11} & y_{21} \\ y_{12} & y_{22} \end{pmatrix}$$

The Kemeny, Morgenstern and Thompson (1956) condition from (*i*) above holds for this simple example if

$$y_{11} + y_{21} > 0,$$

which also holds for output 2, requiring that one of the outputs must be strictly positive. Violation of this restriction implies that each output is equal to zero, which is equivalent to saying that no DMU produces that output and it may be deleted from the matrix.

Condition (*ii*) holds if

$$y_{11} + y_{12} > 0,$$

which also holds for DMU 2, i.e., both DMUs produce at least one output, but not necessarily two. If this condition does not hold, then the associated DMU is producing no outputs, which suggests that the data should be carefully checked.

For our simple example, the first of the input conditions (*iii*) requires that

$$x_{11} + x_{21} > 0,$$

similarly for input 2, requiring that at least one of the DMUs uses one of the inputs. If this does not hold, then neither DMU uses that input and it should be deleted from the X matrix.

Finally, (*iv*) requires that

$$x_{11} + x_{12} > 0,$$

similarly for DMU 2, i.e., each DMU uses at least one input to produce output.

It is straightforward to determine if the input and output matrices satisfy these minimal conditions.

In order to discuss the conditions on outputs under which the output set Y satisfies null jointness, we begin by extending the DEA technology to accommodate bad or undesirable outputs. Denoting bad outputs by

$$b = (b_1, \ldots, b_J) \in \Re_+^J,$$

the output set now reads

$$P(x) = \{(y, b) : x \text{ can produce } y\}, \tag{2.2}$$

and **null jointness**[1] between good and bad output is defined as

$$(y, b) \in P(x) \quad \text{and} \quad b = 0 \text{ imply } y = 0. \tag{2.3}$$

We note that this can be refined to allow for a subvector of y to be nulljoint with a subvector of bad outputs. To formulate a DEA technology that accommodates undesirable outputs assume that data on such outputs for each DMU $k = 1, \ldots, K$ are denoted

$$(b_{k1}, \ldots, b_{kJ}), \quad k = 1, \ldots, K.$$

The model now reads

$$P(x^o) = \left\{ (y, b) : \quad \sum_{k=1}^{K} z_k x_{kn} \leqq x_n^o, \quad n = 1, \ldots, N \right. \tag{2.4}$$

$$\sum_{k=1}^{K} z_k y_{km} \geqq y_m, \quad m = 1, \ldots, M$$

$$\sum_{k=1}^{K} z_k b_{kj} = b_j, \quad j = 1, \ldots, J$$

$$\left. z_k \geqq 0, \quad k = 1, \ldots, K \right\}.$$

This model has $j = 1, \ldots, J$ additional constraints added to the usual input and output constraints. Here these additional constraints are strict equalities (rather than inequalities) which imposes weak rather than strong disposability of good and bad outputs.

Färe and Grosskopf (2004) introduced the following two conditions on the undesirable output data to accommodate null jointness:

$$(v) \sum_{k=1}^{K} b_{kj} > 0, \quad j = 1, \ldots, J \quad (vi) \sum_{j=1}^{J} b_{kj} > 0, \quad k = 1, \ldots, K.$$

$$\tag{2.5}$$

---

[1]This concept was introduced by Shephard and Färe (1974).

If (v) and (vi) are not satisfied and $b_j = 0$, $j = 1, \ldots, J$, then the DEA problem with the extended technology will have all intensity variables equal to zero, i.e., $z_k = 0$, $k = 1, \ldots, K$. In turn $y_m = 0$ for all m, i.e., the problem degenerates. This establishes that (v) and (vi) are sufficient for the extended DEA technology to accommodate null jointness.

As a simple illustration of these conditions assume again that we have two DMUs producing two bad outputs, then the 'bad' matrix may be written

$$B = \begin{pmatrix} b_{11} & b_{21} \\ b_{12} & b_{22} \end{pmatrix}$$

and condition (v) holds provided

$$b_{11} + b_{21} > 0,$$

similarly for bad output 2, thus some of each bad output is produced. Condition (vi) holds provided

$$b_{11} + b_{12} > 0,$$

similarly for DMU 2, thus each DMU produces some bad output.

2.2 Technical Change

In the DEA world technical change is usually estimated using a Malmquist productivity change index. This index, introduced by Caves, Christensen and Diewert (1982), is defined as ratios of Shephard distance functions (1953, 1970). These functions are estimated relative to a frontier technology, such as a DEA technology.

Before we turn to the main topic of this section — namely technical change as embedded in the data matrix M, we recall how the Malmquist index developed.

Assume that we have one DMU producing one output using one input in two time periods $t = 0, 1$. The average productivity in each period is defined as

$$y^o/x^o \quad \text{and} \quad y^1/x^1.$$

The ratio of these is an index of productivity change

$$\frac{y^1/x^1}{y^o/x^o}. \tag{2.6}$$

Multiplying and dividing this ratio of ratios with Shephard output distance function (satisfying CRS) yields

$$\frac{y^1/x^1}{y^o/x^o} \cdot \frac{D_o(1,1)}{D_o(1,1)} = \frac{D_o(x^1, y^1)}{D_o(x^o, y^o)}. \tag{2.7}$$

From this we may generalize and assume that rather than scalar input and output, we may have $x \in \Re_+^N$ and $y \in \Re_+^M$.

The Malmquist productivity change index is also based on distance functions estimated at two (usually adjacent) time periods

$$\left(\frac{D_o^1(x^1, y^1)}{D_o^1(x^o, y^o)} \cdot \frac{D_o^o(x^1, y^1)}{D_o^o(x^o, y^o)} \right)^{1/2} \tag{2.8}$$

where the o and the 1 superscripts on the distance function refer to the data constructing the reference technology, whereas those on the x:s and y:s refer to the period of the data under evaluation. Thus $D_o^1(x^o, y^o)$ is the distance function which evaluates data from period o relative to the technology constructed from period 1. These superscripts could also refer to locations, rather than time periods.

In the Malmquist context, we identify technical change through the distance functions, which can be estimated as output oriented efficiency measures using DEA. We now focus rather on the data itself to identify changes in technology. We begin by assuming that we are given two technology matrices M^o and M^1 where the superscripts again refer to time periods, locations, etc.:

$$M^o = \begin{pmatrix} -x_{11}^o & \cdots & -x_{K1}^o \\ \vdots & \cdots & \vdots \\ -x_{1N}^o & \cdots & -x_{KN}^o \\ y_{11}^o & \cdots & y_{K1}^o \\ \vdots & \cdots & \vdots \\ y_{1M}^o & \cdots & y_{KM}^o \end{pmatrix}$$

$$M^1 = \begin{pmatrix} -x_{11}^1 & \cdots & -x_{K1}^1 \\ \vdots & \cdots & \vdots \\ -x_{1N}^1 & \cdots & -x_{KN}^1 \\ y_{11}^1 & \cdots & y_{K1}^1 \\ \vdots & \cdots & \vdots \\ y_{1M}^1 & \cdots & y_{KM}^1 \end{pmatrix}.$$

We are interested in changes in the technology embedded in these data. We identify three different changes that may occur between these two matrices:[2]

(*i*) the number of columns may change between period 0 and 1
(*ii*) the number of rows may change
(*iii*) the individual entries in the matrices may change

A change in the number of columns between periods identifies exit or entry of DMUs, and changes in rows identifies new and disappearing inputs and outputs. Here we focus on (*iii*), and study changes in the data entries, i.e., the matrix coefficients.

By looking at the difference:

$$\Delta M = M^1 - M^o$$

we may identify whether more or fewer inputs have been employed and whether more or fewer outputs have been produced in period 1 relative to period 0. To provide an example, we assume that we have two DMUs which use one input to produce one output with the following coefficients:

$$M^o = \begin{pmatrix} -1 & -2 \\ 2 & 1 \end{pmatrix}$$

and

$$M^1 = \begin{pmatrix} -1 & -1 \\ 2 & 2 \end{pmatrix}$$

---

[2]See Brozen (1951).

respectively, then ΔM equals

$$\Delta M = \begin{pmatrix} 0 & 1 \\ 0 & 1 \end{pmatrix}.$$

From this we learn that there has been no change in DMU 1 between 0 and 1 while DMU 2 produces one more unit of output using one unit less input. This gives us a disaggregated or micro view of the changes between periods. To get an aggregate estimate of the difference between the matrices one may use a Euclidean norm, which for our example is calculated as

$$\begin{aligned}
& ((-1-(-1))^2 + (2-2)^2)^{1/2} \quad \text{DMU 1} \qquad (2.9)\\
& + ((-1-(-2))^2 + (2-1)^2)^{1/2} \quad \text{DMU 2}\\
& = 0 + 2^{1/2} = 2^{1/2}
\end{aligned}$$

Thus the summary change $\Delta M = 2^{1/2}$. Note that if negative entries in ΔM occur, the (Euclidean) measure is still nonnegative, thus it does not discriminate between technical progress and technical regress.

If one were to estimate the Malmquist productivity change index for our simple example data, DMU 1 would have no productivity change, and DMU 2 would have productivity change index equal to 4, which we leave to the reader for confirmation.

Returning to the analysis of the data matrices, we may ask: how do we identify the DMU which is most efficient in changing their technology over time? One possibility would be to define a Farrell (1957) technical change index based on the ΔM matrix. Assuming that all entries are nonnegative we may compute the following

$$\max \theta \qquad (2.10)$$

$$s.t. \quad \sum_{k=1}^{K} z_k \Delta x_{kn} \leqq \Delta x_{k'n}, \quad n = 1, \ldots, N$$

$$\sum_{k=1}^{K} z_k \Delta y_{km} \geqq \theta \Delta y_{k'm}, \quad m = 1, \ldots, M$$

$$z_k \geqq 0, \qquad k = 1, \ldots, K.$$

for each $k' = 1, \ldots, K$.[3] This efficiency measure would tell us which DMU has been the most efficient in changing the technology.

2.3 Data Translation

When data is ordinal, ordinary DEA models are not appropriate.[4] Here we focus on cardinalizing that data by considering their first order, linear approximation as a suitable transformation of the data. This cardinalization yields a possible change of origin (which we call an additive change) and a possible change in the unit of measurement (which we call a multiplicative change). Our approach is to ask which types of DEA models are invariant with respect to these types of data transformations.[5]

To set the stage assume that we have a model m:

$$m : \Re \to m(p) \in \Re, \tag{2.11}$$

mapping data $p \in \Re$ into $m(p) \in \Re$. We transform the data p into q

$$q = h(p), \tag{2.12}$$

where $h : \Re \to \Re$ is strictly monotonic and continuous.[6] We consider two transformations of the data:

$$h(p) = ap, \quad a > 0 \tag{2.13}$$

and

$$h(p) = ap + b, \quad a, b > 0. \tag{2.14}$$

The second of these transformations follows from a linear transformation of $h(p)$ around p^o. We have

$$h(p) = \frac{dh(p^o)}{dp} \cdot p + h(p^o). \tag{2.15}$$

---

[3] See the appendix following this chapter for these calculations.
[4] Often these are what are sometimes referred to as categorical or environmental variables and have been addressed in various ways, see for example, Banker and Morey (1986a, 1986b).
[5] This section builds on Färe and Grosskopf (2012).
[6] These assumptions suffice for h to have an inverse.

By choosing the coefficients

$$a = \frac{dh(p^o)}{dp} \quad \text{and} \quad b = h(p^o),$$ (2.16)

our linear approximation of the ordinal data becomes an affine data transformation

$$h(p) = ap + b.$$ (2.17)

Next we show that this transformation has cardinal meaning.[7]

For simplicity, assume that we have four data points, $p_i, i = 1, \ldots, 4$ and suppose that this data satisfies the following relationship

$$p_1 - p_2 > p_3 - p_4.$$ (2.18)

Next, suppose that each p_i has been transformed into

$$q_i = ap_i + b, \quad i = 1, \ldots, 4.$$ (2.19)

From the last two expressions we have

$$q_1 - q_2 = ap_1 - b - (ap_2 - b)$$
$$= a(p_1 - p_2)$$
$$> a(p_3 - p_4)$$
$$= ap_3 - ap_4 + b - b$$
$$= q_3 - q_4.$$

Thus it follows that

$$(q_1 - q_2) > (q_3 - q_4) \Leftrightarrow (p_1 - p_2) > (p_3 - p_4)$$ (2.20)

and the differences have a cardinal meaning.

The affine transformation of data was interpreted as a linear approximation of the ordinal data $h(p)$. What does this mean for the data generating process? The linear approximation is a calculus concept, thus the data generating process needs to allow for 'neighborhoods', since calculus

---

[7]Recall that the difference between a utility function, unique up to a monotone transformation (ordinal) and the von Neumann and Morgenstern (1944) utility function, unique up to an affine transformation (cardinal).

is based on limits (and continuity). Thus to accommodate these linear approximations, the ordinal data should be in the form of 'thermometers' rather than integers. For example, if the ordinal data is on a scale from 0 to 5, it should be possible to include a number like π.

Next we turn to the issue of unit invariance. Our model is said to be invariant with respect to a data transformation

$$h(p) = q \tag{2.21}$$

if and only if

$$m(p) = m(h(p)) = m(q), \tag{2.22}$$

i.e., the model m yields the same outcome if p or alternatively $h(p)$ are used as data.

Here we consider two possible transformations of our data:

(i) $h(p) = a(p), a > 0$ and
(ii) $h(p) = ap + b, a > 0, b \in \Re$.

The first transformation allows for changes in the unit of measurement, such as a change from ounces to pounds, while the second transformation also allows changes in the origin, which is useful when the raw data include negative numbers.

Next we analyze changes in the unit of measurement and origin for two DEA type models: the Charnes, Cooper and Rhodes (1978) model and the directional distance function model. We begin with the CCR model, using the input oriented case,[8] namely

$$\min \lambda \tag{2.23}$$

$$\text{s.t.} \quad \sum_{k=1}^{K} z_k x_{kn} \leqq \lambda x_{k'n}, \quad n = 1, \ldots, N,$$

$$\sum_{k=1}^{K} z_k y_{km} \geqq y_{k'm}, \quad m = 1, \ldots, M,$$

$$z_k \geqq 0, \quad k = 1, \ldots, K$$

---

[8] Similar analysis also applies to the output oriented model.

where x_{kn} and y_{km} are observed inputs and outputs and the z_k are intensity variables, here restricted only to be nonnegative, thus constant returns to scale are imposed as in the original CCR model. Here we are evaluating DMU k'.

We now investigate the data transformation $h(p) = ap$ together with the input-oriented CCR model. For illustration we transform the input data, i.e., we introduce

$$h(x_{kn}) = a_n x_{kn}, \quad k = 1, \ldots, K, \quad a_n > 0. \tag{2.24}$$

Inserting this expression into the CCR model yields

$$\min \lambda \tag{2.25}$$

$$\text{s.t.} \quad \sum_{k=1}^{K} z_k (a_n x_{kn}) \leqq \lambda (a_n x_{k'n}), \quad n = 1, \ldots, N,$$

$$\sum_{k=1}^{K} z_k y_{km} \geqq y_{k'm}, \qquad m = 1, \ldots, M,$$

$$z_k \geqq 0 \qquad k = 1, \ldots, K$$

which holds since the a_n terms may be cancelled, reducing this to the original CCR problem. Thus the CCR model is invariant with respect to changes in unit of measurement that are multiplicative transformations.

Note that the intensity variables are not involved in the above argument, thus our invariance results hold with respect to any other restrictions that may be imposed on the z_k variables such as nonincreasing returns to scale $\sum_{k=1}^{K} z_k \leqq 1$ or variable returns to scale $\sum_{k=1}^{K} z_k = 1$.

What is the most general transformation of the data under which the CCR is invariant? To answer this consider, for input n,[9]

$$\sum_{k=1}^{K} z_k h(x_{kn}) \leqq \lambda h(x_{k'n}). \tag{2.26}$$

We need to solve for the $h(\cdot)$ which again is equivalent to the original constraint. Assume that the model is invariant with respect to the above

---

[9]It suffices to focus on one input constraint.

transformation so that

$$\sum_{k=1}^{K} z_k \frac{h(x_{kn})}{h(x_{k'n})} = \sum_{k=1}^{K} z_k \frac{x_{kn}}{x_{k'n}}. \tag{2.27}$$

Note that for some n, the inequality in (2.25) needs to hold with equality, otherwise the minimization problem would not have a solution, since one could then decrease λ.

To solve for $h(.)$, let $k = 1$ be an efficient DMU, then $z_1 = 1$ and $z_k = 0, k = 2, \ldots, K$, thus

$$h(x_{kn}) = \frac{h(x_{k'n})}{x_{k'n}} \cdot x_{kn}, \tag{2.28}$$

and hence for fixed $x_{k'n}$, we can set

$$a_n = \frac{h(x_{k'n})}{x_{k'n}} \tag{2.29}$$

therefore,

$$h(x_{kn}) = a_n x_{kn}. \tag{2.30}$$

Thus we have shown that the most general data transformation under which the CCR model is invariant is

$$h(x_{kn}) = a_n x_{kn}. \tag{2.31}$$

Moreover under this condition, we have in the general model that

$$m(a_n x_{kn}) = m(x_{kn}), \tag{2.32}$$

showing that the model must be homogeneous of degree zero in its data x_{kn}, which is satisfied by the CCR model.

We turn now to affine transformations, i.e.,

$$h(x_{kn}) = a_n x_{kn} + b_n, \quad a_n > 0, \quad b_n \in \mathfrak{R}. \tag{2.33}$$

We analyze this transformation in the framework of a directional input distance function,[10] introduced by Luenberger (1992), and estimated in an

---

[10]The reader may consider repeating the analysis for an output directional distance function and output data transformation.

activity analysis framework as:

$$\max \beta \tag{2.34}$$

$$\text{s.t.} \quad \sum_{k=1}^{K} z_k (x_{kn}) \leqq x_{k'n} - \beta g_n, \quad n = 1, \ldots, N,$$

$$\sum_{k=1}^{K} z_k y_{km} \geqq y_{k'm}, \qquad m = 1, \ldots, M,$$

$$z_k \geqq 0 \qquad k = 1, \ldots, K$$

$$\sum_{k=1}^{K} z_k = 1,$$

where the last expression imposes variable returns to scale (VRS). As will become evident, this assumption is essential to show invariance.

The $g = (g_1, \ldots, g_N) \geqq 0, g \neq 0$, is the directional input vector which specifies the direction in which the input data is projected onto the technology frontier. So instead of a proportional contraction of the input vector, we are allowing for non-proportional reductions of the input vector.

If we insert the transformed input data into the model we have

$$\max \beta \tag{2.35}$$

$$\text{s.t.} \quad \sum_{k=1}^{K} z_k (a_n x_{kn} + b_n) \leqq a_n x_{k'n} + b_n - \beta a_n g_n, \quad n = 1, \ldots, N,$$

$$\sum_{k=1}^{K} z_k y_{km} \geqq y_{k'm}, \qquad m = 1, \ldots, M,$$

$$z_k \geqq 0 \qquad k = 1, \ldots, K$$

$$\sum_{k=1}^{K} z_k = 1.$$

Note that since the unit of measurement of inputs changes from x_{kn} to $a_n x_{kn}$, the directional vector must also change from g_n to $a_n g_n$, maintaining the same unit of measurement for inputs and directions.

As before we can focus on one of the input constraints, say the nth, noting that

$$\sum_{k=1}^{K} z_k (a_n x_{kn} + b_n) \leqq a_n x_{k'n} + b_n - \beta a_n g_n \qquad (2.36)$$

may be rewritten as

$$a_n \sum_{k=1}^{K} z_k x_{kn} + b_n \sum_{k=1}^{K} z_k \leqq a_n x_{k'n} + b_n - \beta a_n g_n. \qquad (2.37)$$

Since we have assumed VRS, $\sum_{k=1}^{K} z_k = 1$, which simplifies our input constraint to

$$a_n \sum_{k=1}^{K} z_k x_{kn} \leqq a_n (x_{k'n} - \beta g_n), \qquad (2.38)$$

thus

$$\sum_{k=1}^{K} z_k x_{kn} \leqq x_{k'n} - \beta g_n, \qquad (2.39)$$

which is the original input constraint, demonstrating that the directional (DEA) input distance function is invariant with respect to affine data transformations, assuming VRS.

Does this result hold under constant returns to scale? Again we focus on one input constraint, for input n

$$\sum_{k=1}^{K} z_k h(x_{kn}) \leqq h(x_{k'n}) - \beta f(g_n), \qquad (2.40)$$

where $f(g_n)$ is a function equating the unit of measurement with $h(x_{k'n})$. Since at least one DMU is efficient, say DMU 1, then $z_1 = 1$ and $z_k = 0$, $k = 2, \ldots, K$.

Assuming invariance we have

$$\frac{h(x_{1n})}{f(g_n)} - \frac{h(x_{k'n})}{f(g_n)} = \frac{x_{1n}}{g_n} - \frac{x_{k'n}}{g_n} \qquad (2.41)$$

or

$$h(x_{1n}) = h(x_{k'n}) + \frac{x_{1n} f(g_n)}{g_n} - \frac{x_{k'n} f(g_n)}{g_n}. \tag{2.42}$$

Now take

$$a_n = \frac{f(g_n)}{g_n}, \quad b_n = h(x_{k'n}) - \frac{x_{k'n} f(g_n)}{g_n} \tag{2.43}$$

then

$$h(x_{1n}) = a_n x_{1n} + b_n, \tag{2.44}$$

showing that the affine data transformation is the most general transformation for the DEA directional distance function, under VRS or CRS.

2.4   Appendix: Distance Functions

In this appendix we introduce and briefly discuss the distance functions employed in this monograph. We begin with the most general form — the additive or directional distance functions. We then turn to the multiplicative or Shephard distance functions, which are in fact special cases of the directional distance functions.

Recall that input vectors $x \in \Re_+^N$ are used to produce output vectors $y \in \Re_+^M$, with the technology equivalently represented by

$$T = \{(x, y) : x \text{ can produce } y\}, \quad \text{the technology set}$$
$$P(x) = \{y : (x, y) \in T\}, \qquad \text{the output set}$$
$$L(y) = \{x : (x, y) \in T\}, \qquad \text{the input set.}$$

Denote the vector along which an input/output vector is projected onto the frontier of the technology set by

$$g = (g_x, g_y) \in \Re_+^N \times \Re_+^M, \quad g \neq 0. \tag{2.45}$$

The directional technology distance function is defined by[11]

$$\vec{D}_T(x, y; g) = \sup\{\beta : (x - \beta g_x, y + \beta g_y) \in T\}. \tag{2.46}$$

---

[11]This function was introduced by R.G. Luenberger, see e.g., Luenberger (1992, 1995).

This function projects (x, y) onto the frontier of T in the direction $g = (g_x, g_y)$, where g_x is subtracted from x and g_y is added to y. Given 'some' disposability of inputs and outputs[12] (strong disposability of inputs and outputs is sufficient) this distance function completely characterizes T, i.e.,

$$\vec{D}_T(x, y; g) \geqq 0 \Leftrightarrow (x, y) \in T. \quad \textbf{Representation} \qquad (2.47)$$

This function also inherits the conditions imposed on T, see Chambers, Chung and Färe (1998).

When estimating this function, one may choose g using 'common sense',[13] or endogenize it, see Färe, Grosskopf and Whittaker (2013).

If we restrict $g_x = 0$, we then have what we call an output directional distance function

$$\vec{D}_T(x, y; 0, g_y) = \vec{D}_o(x, y; g_y) = \sup\{\beta : (y + \beta g_y) \in P(x)\} \quad (2.48)$$

and if we instead restrict $g_y = 0$, we have a directional input distance function

$$\vec{D}_T(x, y; g_x, 0) = \vec{D}_i(x, y; g_x) = \sup\{\beta : (x - \beta g_x) \in L(y)\}. \quad (2.49)$$

These functions are complete representations of the output and input sets, respectively:[14]

$$\vec{D}_o(x, y; g_y) \geqq 0 \Leftrightarrow y \in P(x), \quad \textbf{Representation}$$

and

$$\vec{D}_i(x, y; g_x) \geqq 0 \Leftrightarrow x \in L(y), \quad \textbf{Representation}.$$

We refer to these functions as additive since inputs (outputs) are contracted (expanded) additively in their definitions.

---

[12]The weakest form of disposability for representation to hold is called g-disposability.

[13]For example, one may choose a direction consistent with a welfare function, a fixed direction (which facilitates aggregation), the direction of the data (which yields a proportional scaling), among other choices.

[14]Free disposability of outputs suffices for the output distance function and free disposability of inputs for the input distance function.

Shephard's (1953, 1970) output and input distance functions are defined 'multiplicatively', expanding and contracting radially toward the frontier of the output or input set, respectively. For Shephard type distance functions, there is in general no distance function defined on the technology set T.[15]

The input distance function is defined as (Shephard, 1953)

$$D_i(y, x) = \sup\{\lambda : x/\lambda \in L(y)\} \tag{2.50}$$

and the output distance function is defined as (Shephard, 1970)

$$D_o(x, y) = \inf\{\theta : y/\theta \in P(x)\}. \tag{2.51}$$

Each of these functions characterize the technology, $L(y)$ and $P(x)$, respectively:[16]

$$D_i(y, x) \geqq 1 \Leftrightarrow x \in L(y), \quad \textbf{Representation}$$

and

$$D_o(x, y) \leqq 1 \Leftrightarrow y \in P(x), \quad \textbf{Representation}$$

Under CRS, we have

$$D_i(y, x) = 1/D_o(x, y), \tag{2.52}$$

which also is a characterization of CRS.

If we set $g_y = y, g_x = 0$, we can derive a relation between the directional and Shephard output distance functions

$$\vec{D}_o(x, y; y) = (1/D_o(x, y)) - 1 \tag{2.53}$$

and similarly on the input side, if we set $g_x = x, g_y = 0$, we have

$$\vec{D}_i(x, y; x) = 1 - (1/D_i(y, x)). \tag{2.54}$$

---

[15]See Chambers and Färe (1994) for an exception.
[16]Weak disposability of inputs (outputs) is necessary and sufficient for these to hold, see Färe and Primont (1995).

Proofs of the last two statements are found in Färe and Grosskopf (2004). The following Figure 2.1 found in the aforementioned reference summarizes the relationships among these distance functions.

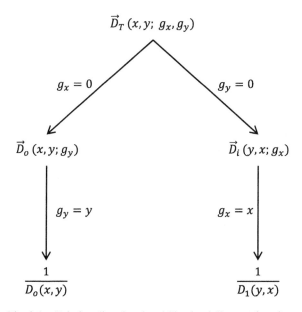

Fig. 2.1. Relating directional and Shephard distance functions.

Chapter 3

DEA and Intensity Variables

The intensity variables in DEA originally were restricted to be nonnegative,[1] and the focus was on their role in constructing the technology and identifying peer DMUs. It was known that the resulting technology satisfied constant returns to scale. Interestingly, in much earlier work using linear programming models of technology, Sydney Afriat (1972) showed that by restricting the intensity variables to sum to one (as well as nonnegative), variable returns to scale (VRS) could be modeled. Similarly, technology could be restricted to exhibit nonincreasing returns to scale by restricting the sum of the intensity variables to be less than or equal to one. Färe, Grosskopf and Logan (1983) used the nested nature of these restrictions to analyze returns to scale in DEA. The more familiar Banker, Charnes and Cooper (1984) (BCC) model followed in 1984.

In the DEA literature other forms of restrictions on the intensity variables have been introduced, see e.g., Cooper, Seiford and Zhu (2004) for a survey of the topic often dubbed 'weight restrictions'.

Here we take a different look at the intensity variables following work in financial economics, and use the duals of these variables to estimate the 'value' of a DMU. Before proceeding, we take a detour to clarify what we mean here by duality and how that differs from its traditional interpretation in production theory as developed by Shephard (1953, 1970). We begin this chapter with a short section on Shephard's duality theory. This is followed

---

[1] In financial economics, these variables are not restricted to be nonnegative. Instead they are elements in $\Re^K$ rather than $\Re_+^K$, which allows for short sales.

by a study of the adjoint transformation of the technology matrix, providing a basis for the next two sections.

We include a section on the Diet Problem to show how this classical linear programming problem is related to DEA, again utilizing the adjoint transformation of the technology matrix, which is also employed when we finally turn to pricing DMUs.

3.1 On Shephard's Duality Theory

To illustrate the difference between the duality familiar from linear programming to that in production theory we start by presenting Shephard's original duality between cost and production, Shephard (1953). Recall that the input set maps output vectors $y \in \Re_+^M$ into input requirements, i.e., sets of input vectors $x \in \Re_+^N$ required to produce y.

$$L(y) = \{x : x \text{ can produce } y\}. \qquad (3.1)$$

Denote input prices by $w \in \Re_+^N$, then the cost function is defined as

$$C(y, w) = \min_x \{wx : x \in L(y)\}. \qquad (3.2)$$

For the minimum to exist, in general, requires that prices be strictly positive, and $L(y)$ closed and nonempty.[2]

We refer to $L(y)$ as a subset of the primal or quantity space. The dual technology is a subset of the dual or price space. It is defined in terms of the cost function:

$$\pounds(y, w, c) = \{w : C(y, w) \leqq c\}, \qquad (3.3)$$

where c is a given cost.

The duality between the primal and dual technologies may be expressed in terms of distance functions defined over them. Recall from Chapter 2 that the input distance function is a complete representation of the input set, i.e.,

$$D_i(y, x) \leqq 1 \Leftrightarrow x \in L(y). \qquad (3.4)$$

---

[2]E.g., if $L(y) = \{(x_1, x_2) : x_1 x_2 \geqq y\}$, i.e., the technology is Cobb–Douglas, then clearly a minimum does not exist if one price is zero; the isoquants approach the axes asymptotically.

Furthermore, we note that the cost function is a distance function in price space. We begin to show this by noting that

$$C(y, \lambda w) = \lambda C(y, w), \quad \lambda > 0, \tag{3.5}$$

i.e., the cost function is homogeneous of degree $+1$ in input prices. Using this we obtain:

$$\inf\{\lambda : w/\lambda \in \pounds(y, w, c)\} = \inf\{\lambda : C(y, w/\lambda) \leqq c\} \tag{3.6}$$
$$= \inf\{\lambda : C(y, w/c) \leqq \lambda\}$$
$$= C(y, w/c).$$

And for nonnegative prices, with strong disposability of prices we have

$$C(y, w) \leqq c \Leftrightarrow w \in \pounds(y, w, c), \tag{3.7}$$

i.e., the cost function is a complete representation of the dual price technology, $\pounds(y, w, c)$.

The primal and dual distance functions are combined in deriving the Mahler (1939) inequality, namely

$$C(y, w) \leqq wx \quad \text{for all } x \in L(y), \tag{3.8}$$

noting that

$$(x/D_i(y, x)) \in L(y) \tag{3.9}$$

and substituting we arrive at the desired result

$$C(y, w) \leqq \frac{wx}{D_i(y, x)}, \tag{3.10}$$

showing how the primal and dual representations of the technology can be expressed by the cost function and the distance function. Rearranging this expression yields the basis for what is known as the Farrell decomposition of cost efficiency.[3]

Under convexity of $L(y)$, it follows that

$$C(y, w) = \min_x \frac{wx}{D_i(y, x)} \tag{3.11}$$

---

[3]This is usually stated as $wx/C(y, w) = D_i(y, x) + AE_i$, where the last term is a residual referred to as allocative efficiency.

and

$$D_i(y, x) = \min_{w} \frac{wx}{C(y, w)}. \tag{3.12}$$

Again, the cost function is a distance function in the dual price space, and by the last equality we note that the input distance function is a cost function in the same space. Thus both functions have dual interpretations as cost and distance functions.

From Chapter 1, the DEA/Activity Analysis model of the input set takes the form

$$L(y^o) = \left\{ (x_1, \ldots, x_N) : \sum_{k=1}^{K} z_k x_{kn} \leqq x_n, \quad n = 1, \ldots, N, \tag{3.13} \right.$$

$$\sum_{k=1}^{K} z_k y_{km} \geqq y_m^o, \quad m = 1, \ldots, M,$$

$$\left. z_k \geqq 0, \quad k = 1, \ldots, K \right\}.$$

Again from Chapter 1, we know that the efficient subset of $L(y^o)$ is bounded, thus since the DEA technology is closed, the closure of this set is compact and is included in $L(y^o)$. This implies that some prices may be equal to zero, thus we let $w \in \Re_+^N$ and define

$$C(y^o, w) = \min_{x} wx \quad \text{s.t. } x \in L(y^o), \tag{3.14}$$

or in terms of the DEA inequalities

$$C(y^o, w) = \min_{x} wx \tag{3.15}$$

$$s.t. \quad \sum_{k=1}^{K} z_k x_{kn} \leqq x_n, \quad n = 1, \ldots, N,$$

$$\sum_{k=1}^{K} z_k y_{km} \geqq y_m^o, \quad m = 1, \ldots, M,$$

$$z_k \geqq 0, \quad k = 1, \ldots, K.$$

Note that minimizing over inputs implies that the intensity variables, $z_k, k = 1, \ldots, K$ become choice variables as well. Thus one may change the cost minimization problem and ask 'what are the best choices of $z_k, k = 1, \ldots, K$?'

Hence, given prices of the intensity variables $(q_1, \ldots, q_K) \in \Re_+^K$, what is the least cost way of using the DMUs. We can write this as

$$\min qz \tag{3.16}$$

$$s.t. \quad \sum_{k=1}^{K} z_k x_{kn} \leqq x_n^o, \quad n = 1, \ldots, N,$$

$$\sum_{k=1}^{K} z_k y_{km} \geqq y_m^o, \quad m = 1, \ldots, M,$$

$$z_k \geqq 0, \quad k = 1, \ldots, K.$$

Written as a function we have

$$Q(x^o, y^o, q) = \min_z qz \tag{3.17}$$

$$s.t. \quad \sum_{k=1}^{K} z_k x_{kn} \leqq x_n^o, \quad n = 1, \ldots, N,$$

$$\sum_{k=1}^{K} z_k y_{km} \geqq y_m^o, \quad m = 1, \ldots, M,$$

$$z_k \geqq 0, \quad k = 1, \ldots, K,$$

which is the 'linear programming' minimization problem. Hence the focus here is on the intensity variables $z_k, k = 1, \ldots, K$.

3.2 Adjoint Transformations in DEA

In the last section, we showed how the duality between input quantities and input prices was developed by Shephard (1953). Here we consider the more general case including both inputs and outputs with an emphasis on the DEA technology. Specifically, we introduce the adjoint transformation associated with this technology. Recall the technology matrix M consisting of input and output quantities. Each column vector represents one DMU, and each row vector is associated with a particular input or output, thus

$$
M = \begin{pmatrix}
-x_{11} & \cdots & -x_{k1} & \cdots & -x_{K1} \\
\vdots & \vdots & \vdots & \vdots & \vdots \\
-x_{1N} & \cdots & -x_{kN} & \cdots & -x_{KN} \\
y_{11} & \cdots & y_{k1} & \cdots & y_{K1} \\
\vdots & \vdots & \vdots & \vdots & \vdots \\
y_{1M} & \cdots & y_{kM} & \cdots & y_{KM}
\end{pmatrix}.
$$

In the DEA world, for each DMU there is a given nonnegative intensity variable $z_k \geq 0, k = 1, \ldots, K$ or $z \in \Re_+^K$. If these are restricted only to be nonnegative, the resulting DEA technology will exhibit CRS (constant returns to scale). The intensity variables serve to map the technology matrix M into input–output space:

$$
Mz \in \Re_-^N \times \Re_+^M, \quad z \in \Re_+^K, \tag{3.18}
$$

with the following technology set:

$$
T = \left\{ (x, y) : Mz \geq (-x, y), z \in \Re_+^K \right\} \tag{3.19}
$$

or in terms of inequalities[4]

$$
T = \Bigg\{ (x, y) : \sum_{k=1}^{K} z_k x_{kn} \leq x_n, \quad n = 1, \ldots, N, \tag{3.20}
$$

$$
\sum_{k=1}^{K} z_k y_{km} \geq y_m, \quad m = 1, \ldots, M,
$$

$$
z_k \geq 0, \quad k = 1, \ldots, K \Bigg\}.
$$

Dual to input quantities are input prices and dual to output quantities are output prices. Dual to the intensity variables are their 'prices', here denoted

---

[4]Note that we are a bit inconsistent with inputs, sometimes they are nonpositive and sometimes nonnegative. This is resolved by reversing the inequalities, however, inputs are typically physically nonnegative units in DEA.

by $q \in \mathfrak{R}_+^K$. These prices are frequently associated with the Diet Problem in linear programming[5] or with security prices in financial economics.[6]

Given these prices, the adjoint transformation in the dual (price) space may be defined as

$$M \begin{pmatrix} w \\ p \end{pmatrix} \in \mathfrak{R}_+^K, \quad (w, p) \in \mathfrak{R}_+^N \times \mathfrak{R}_+^M$$

with the following dual price technology

$$\mathfrak{I} = \left\{ q : -\sum_{n=1}^{N} x_{kn} w_n + \sum_{m=1}^{M} y_{km} p_m \geqq q_k, \forall (w, p) \in \mathfrak{R}_+^N \times \mathfrak{R}_+^M \right\}.$$

$$(3.21)$$

Our discussion may be summarized in a figure, which is our interpretation of Figure 3.1 in Magill and Quinzii (1996).

Primal (Quantity) Space

$z \in \mathbb{R}_+^K$ $\xrightarrow{\quad M \quad}$ $(-x, y) \in \mathbb{R}_+^N \times \mathbb{R}_+^M$

Dual $\quad\quad$ Dual

$q \in \mathbb{R}_+^K$ $\xleftarrow{\quad M' \quad}$ $(w, p) \in \mathbb{R}_+^N \times \mathbb{R}_+^M$

Dual (Price) Space

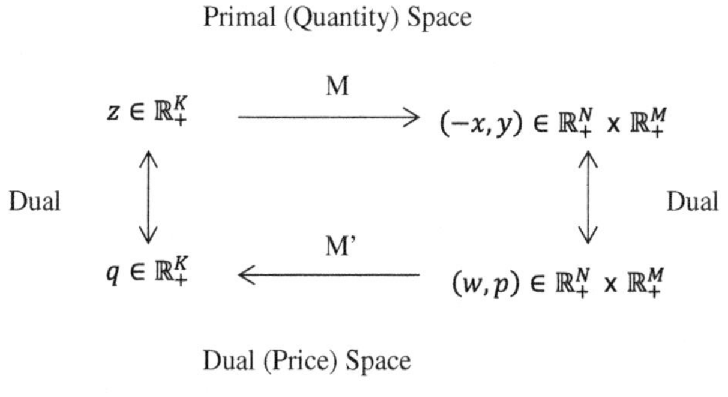

Fig. 3.1. Adjoint transformations: Primal and dual technologies.

The intensity variables in the primal space map the DMU's M into input–output space. In the dual space the adjoint transformation, the transpose of M maps input/output prices into the prices of the DMU's, dual to the intensity variables.

---

[5] See e.g., Gale (1960).
[6] See e.g., Magill and Quinzii (1996).

3.3   The Diet Problem

The diet problem has become 'the classical illustration of linear programming.' Gale (1960, p. 1), but has to a great degree escaped attention from DEA analysts.[7] In this section we look at the classical problem from a DEA perspective. We show that the dual to the diet problem is dual to revenue or profit maximization problem (depending on the formulation) in DEA. In terms of the duality figure in our previous section, the duality is between the SW and NE corners.

In DEA the intensity variables tell us 'how much' of a given DMU is participating in a solution to one of many optimization problems. In the diet problem, DMUs are food groups like bread, milk, etc. Each food group delivers various types of nutrition (outputs) such as calories, vitamins, etc. The optimization problem is to find the minimal cost of food groups or DMUs that delivers a 'healthy meal.'

To illustrate, we borrow an example from Baldani *et al.* (1996) and assume that we have two DMUs: $DMU\,1 = $ milk, $DMU\,2 = $ cereal, which produce calcium and vitamin A, i.e.,

	milk	cereal
Vitamin A	y_{11}	y_{21}
Calcium	y_{12}	y_{22}

Assuming that Vitamin A should exceed some minimum level y_1 and Calcium should exceed some minimum level y_2 for a healthy meal, what is the cheapest way to provide that meal? i.e., what are the intensity variables z_1 and z_2 that minimize the cost? Recall that the price of the intensity variables are q_1 and q_2 which is the cost of a serving of milk and cereal, respectively.

Thus

$$\min_{z_1, z_2} \quad q_1 z_1 + q_2 z_2 \qquad (3.22)$$

$$s.t. \quad z_1 y_{11} + z_2 y_{21} \geqq y_1$$

$$z_1 y_{12} + z_2 y_{22} \geqq y_2$$

$$z_1, z_2 \geqq 0.$$

---

[7]One exception is Färe, Grosskopf and Margaritis (2011).

This optimization problem takes us from the NW corner to the SW corner in the duality figure. To return to the NW from the SW corner, we may formulate the following La Grange problem[8]

$$\pounds = q_1 z_1 + q_2 z_2 + \mu_1(y_1 - z_1 y_{11} - z_2 y_{21}) + \mu_2(y_2 - z_1 y_{12} - z_2 y_{22})$$

$$= q_1 z_1 + q_2 z_2 + \mu_1 y_1 - \mu_1 z_1 y_{11} - \mu_1 z_2 y_{21} + \mu_2 y_2$$

$$- \mu_2 z_1 y_{12} - \mu_2 z_2 y_{22}$$

$$= \mu_1 y_1 + \mu_2 y_2 + z_1(q_1 - \mu_1 y_{11} - \mu_2 y_{12}) + z_2(q_2 - \mu_1 y_{21} - \mu_2 y_{22})$$

$$(3.23)$$

or as a dual linear programming problem

$$\max_{\mu_1, \mu_2} \quad \mu_1 y_1 + \mu_2 y_2 \qquad\qquad (3.24)$$

$$s.t. \quad \mu_1 y_{11} + \mu_2 y_{12} \leqq q_1$$

$$\mu_1 y_{21} + \mu_2 y_{22} \leqq q_2$$

$$\mu_1, \mu_2 \geqq 0.$$

The minimization problem takes us from NW to SW whereas the maximization problem takes us back from SW to NW.

To relate the diet problem to a typical DEA problem, first note that the $\mu_m, m = 1, 2$ are the prices of the outputs, which in turn are the shadow prices in the Lagrangian problem with respect to $y_m, m = 1, 2$. Thus the objective function is to maximize revenue with respect to prices. The dual to such a problem is optimization over quantities, given prices, i.e., maximize revenue with respect to output quantities, the latter of which is a traditional DEA type problem.

Specifically, the DEA revenue maximization problem with respect to quantities may be written as

$$\max_{y_1, y_2, z} \quad p_1 y_1 + p_2 y_2 \qquad\qquad (3.25)$$

$$s.t. \quad z_1 y_{11} + z_2 y_{21} \geqq y_1$$

$$z_1 y_{12} + z_2 y_{22} \geqq y_2$$

$$z_1, z_2 \geqq 0.$$

---

[8]Again we follow Baldani, Bradfield and Turner (1996).

However, one may also need to put an upper bound on the intensity variables (the $z's$) to find a solution. In the DEA world, this is typically introduced indirectly through input constraints. Thus if we extend the diet problem to allow for the outputs to be produced from a single input[9] for each DMU, i.e., x_1 and x_2, then the revenue maximization problem is soluble as

$$\max_{y_1, y_2, z} \quad p_1 y_1 + p_2 y_2 \tag{3.26}$$

$$s.t. \quad z_1 y_{11} + z_2 y_{21} \geqq y_1$$

$$z_1 y_{12} + z_2 y_{22} \geqq y_2$$

$$z_1 x_1 + z_2 x_2 \leqq x$$

$$z_1, z_2 \geqq 0,$$

where x may be given as an observed DMU's input use.

Thus following Färe, Grosskopf and Margaritis (2011), we can extend the diet problem to include inputs. We begin by considering the DEA profit maximization problem. Recall that input prices are denoted by $w \in \Re_+^N$ and output prices by $p \in \Re_+^M$, then maximum profit may be found as the solution to the following DEA type linear programming problem[10]

$$\max_{x, y} \quad py - wx \tag{3.27}$$

$$s.t. \quad \sum_{k=1}^{K} z_k x_{kn} \leqq x_n, \quad n = 1, \dots, N$$

$$\sum_{k=1}^{K} z_k y_{km} \geqq y_m, \quad m = 1, \dots, M$$

$$z_k \geqq 0, \quad k = 1, \dots, K.$$

---

[9]This assumption is for simplicity, multiple inputs may be included.

[10]This formulation exhibits constant returns to scale, which under competition yields maximum zero profit. This is unimportant for our objective here, which is to find the relationship between the diet problem and DEA.

Or in matrix notation

$$\max \ py - wx \tag{3.28}$$
$$s.t. \ Xz \leqq x$$
$$Yz \geqq y$$
$$z \in \mathfrak{R}_+^K.$$

The Lagrangian formulation associated with this problem is

$$\max_{x,y,\lambda,\mu} \ py - wx + \lambda(Xz - x) + \mu(y - Yz), \tag{3.29}$$

where $\lambda = (\lambda_1, \ldots, \lambda_N)$ and $\mu = (\mu_1, \ldots, \mu_M)$ are the Lagrangian multipliers.

The extended diet problem which includes inputs and outputs is given by

$$\min qz \tag{3.30}$$
$$s.t. \ \sum_{k=1}^{K} z_k x_{kn} \leqq x_n^o, \quad n = 1, \ldots, N$$
$$\sum_{k=1}^{K} z_k y_{km} \geqq y_m^o, \quad m = 1, \ldots, M$$
$$z_k \geqq 0, \quad k = 1, \ldots, K$$

or in matrix form

$$\min qz \tag{3.31}$$
$$s.t. \ Xz \leqq x^o$$
$$Yz \geqq y^o$$
$$z \in \mathfrak{R}_+^K$$

where (x^o, y^o) defines a 'healthy meal'. In terms of the Lagrange problem this becomes

$$\min_{z,\hat{\lambda},\hat{\mu}} qz + \hat{\lambda}(Xz - x^o) + \hat{\mu}(y^o - Yz), \tag{3.32}$$

where $\hat{\lambda} = (\hat{\lambda}_1, \ldots, \hat{\lambda}_N)$ and $\hat{\mu} = (\hat{\mu}_1, \ldots, \hat{\mu}_M)$ are the Lagrangian multipliers. This problem can be transformed into its dual form, by

$$= \min_{z,\lambda,\hat{\mu}} \hat{\mu} y^o - \hat{\lambda} x^o + (q + \hat{\lambda} X - \hat{\mu} Y)z. \tag{3.33}$$

Recall that the dual variables $\hat{\lambda}$, $\hat{\mu}$ are prices, so we may set $\hat{\lambda} = w$ and $\hat{\mu} = p$, thus we have

$$\min_{z,p,w} py^o - wx^o + (q + wX - pY)z. \tag{3.34}$$

If we compare this problem to the Lagrangian formulation of the DEA profit maximization problem

$$\max_{x,y,\lambda,\mu} py - wx + \lambda(Xz - x) + \mu(y - Yz) \tag{3.35}$$

we see that they are duals. In the duality figure, this dual relation is between the SW corner and the NE corner.

3.4   Pricing Decision Making Units

In this section we lay out the theoretical foundation for pricing DMUs following Färe, Grosskopf and Margaritis (2012). We build on the idea of pricing securities, well known in the financial economics literature, as in Magill and Quinzii (1996). The idea consists of studying the adjoint transformation associated with the DEA technology. Specifically the intensity variables are used to map the DEA technology matrix into input–output space. This is illustrated in the duality figure in Section 2 of this chapter.

Assume that the technology matrix M is known, then its adjoint transformation maps input–output prices (w, p) into the prices of the intensity variables, i.e.,

$$M' \begin{pmatrix} w \\ p \end{pmatrix} = (wp)M = q$$

where

$$q_k = \sum_{m=1}^{M} p_m y_{km} - \sum_{n=1}^{N} w_n x_{kn}, \quad k = 1, \ldots, K. \tag{3.36}$$

Thus the unit price of intensity variable k or DMU k is its revenue minus cost or its profit, so pricing DMUs is achieved by evaluating their profits.

To illustrate our result, consider the inner product of $q \in \Re_+^K$ and $z \in \Re_+^K$,

$$qz = \sum_{k=1}^{K} q_k z_k. \tag{3.37}$$

Thus for any $z_k \geq 0$, setting it equal to one and the other elements equal to zero, shows that q_k is the unit price of that DMU. Thus our pricing model applies to DMUs with intensity variables whose value is unity, which in the Farrell framework refers to efficient DMUs. To extend our model to those DMUs which are not efficient, we look at inefficiency in a Farrell input-oriented framework.

Let the input set for DMU k be given by

$$L(y^{k'}) = \left\{ x : \sum_{k=1}^{K} z_k x_{kn} \leqq x_n, \quad n = 1, \ldots, N \right. \tag{3.38}$$

$$\sum_{k=1}^{K} z_k y_{km} \geqq y_m, \quad m = 1, \ldots, M$$

$$\left. z_k \geqq 0, \quad k = 1, \ldots, K \right\}.$$

$L(y^{k'})$ satisfies strong disposability of inputs and outputs as well as CRS. We evaluate its input vector $x^{k'}$ with an input-oriented Farrell (1957) technical efficiency measure

$$F(x^{k'}, y^{k'}) = \min \lambda \tag{3.39}$$

$$s.t. \quad \sum_{k=1}^{K} z_k x_{kn} \leqq \lambda x_{k'n}, \quad n = 1, \ldots, N$$

$$\sum_{k=1}^{K} z_k y_{km} \geqq y_{k'm}, \quad m = 1, \ldots, M$$

$$z_k \geqq 0, \quad k = 1, \ldots, K.$$

If k' is efficient its score is one, and the problem above provides its value. If it is inefficient, then $z_{k'} = 0$ and $x^{k'}$ will be projected onto the isoquant[11] of $L(y^{k'})$ which consists of convex combinations of other DMUs whose intensity variables are positive. As an illustration we include the example from Färe, Grosskopf and Margaritis (2012). They assume that there are three DMUs which use two inputs to produce a single output, with the data given below.

	DMU1	DMU2	DMU3
x_1	1	2	2
x_2	2	1	2
y	5	5	5

The data are plotted in Figure 3.2 below, which includes the resultant isoquant.

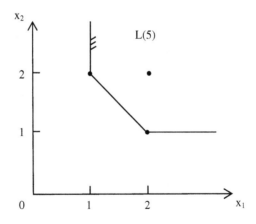

Fig. 3.2.   Technology with 3 DMUs.

DMUs 1 and 2 'span' the input set $L(5)$, and thus are efficient in the sense of Farrell. DMU 3 is interior to the input set and can be radially contracted while remaining in the input set, hence it is Farrell inefficient.

---

[11]The isoquant is defined as ISOQ $L(y) = \{x : x \in L(y), \lambda x \notin L(y), \lambda < 1\}$.

DMU 3's efficiency score is computed as the solution to the following problem

$$\min \lambda \qquad (3.40)$$

$$s.t. \quad 1z_1 + 2z_2 + 2z_3 \leqq \lambda 2$$

$$2z_1 + 1z_2 + 2z_3 \leqq \lambda 2$$

$$5z_1 + 5z_2 + 5z_3 \geqq 5$$

$$z_1, z_2, z_3 \geqq 0.$$

The solution to this problem is

$$\lambda^* = 0.75$$

$$z_1^* = 0.5$$

$$z_2^* = 0.5$$

$$z_3^* = 0.$$

Thus the efficiency score is 0.75 and the 'virtual' inputs, i.e., the inputs at the point on the isoquant to which DMU 3's input bundle would be projected, are

$$x_{31}^* = 1 \cdot 0.5 + 2 \cdot 0.5 + 2 \cdot 0 = 1.5 \qquad (3.41)$$

$$x_{32}^* = 2 \cdot 0.5 + 1 \cdot 0.5 + 2 \cdot 0 = 1.5$$

and the virtual output is

$$y^* = 5 \cdot 0.5 + 5 \cdot 0.5 + 5 \cdot 0 = 5 \qquad (3.42)$$

which is equal to its observed output, which is as it should be since the input oriented efficiency measure does not alter output levels.

Assume as in Färe *et al.* (2012) that input and output prices are

$$p = w_1 = w_2 = 1,$$

then

$$q_3^* = 1 \cdot 5 - 1 \cdot 1.5 - 1 \cdot 1.5 = 2. \qquad (3.43)$$

Thus the price of the virtual DMU 3 is one unit higher than its original price

$$q_3 = 1 \cdot 5 - 1 \cdot 2 - 1 \cdot 2 = 1. \qquad (3.44)$$

DMU 3 becomes worth one more unit when it becomes efficient.

Chapter 4

DEA and Directional Distance Functions

In Chapter 4 we undertake an in-depth study of directional distance functions and how they apply to DEA.

We begin the chapter with a discussion of the directional vectors and how they influence the DEA scores for inefficient DMUs. We next consider the role of the direction vectors when the goal is to aggregate across DMUs. Here we show that aggregation is facilitated when the DMUs are given the same direction vector, in particular the unit direction.

The concluding section addresses the choice of direction in general, and how to endogenize that choice in particular. This leads us to a discussion of directional distance functions and their indication properties, i.e., the subsets of the technology to which the DMUs under evaluation are projected. We also show how the endogenization of the directions are related to slack-based directional distance functions.

An appendix including an indication theorem concludes.

4.1 Directional Vectors

In the Appendix to Chapter 2 we discuss the general theory of distance functions including the Shephard input and output distance functions as well as directional distance functions. We note that the directional distance functions are 'additive' whereas the Shephard distance functions are of a multiplicative nature. As a consequence the directional distance functions by definition possess a translation property while the Shephard distance functions exhibit homogeneity instead. In Chapter 2 we discuss what data transformations are feasible in a DEA framework given these properties.

In this section we show how these functions may be estimated using DEA. We remind the reader that in the directional case, the researcher chooses the direction in which DMUs will be projected to the frontier, while in the multiplicative case that direction is given by the data under evaluation. That direction is a special case for the directional distance function.

Recall that the DEA technology set is

$$
T = \left\{ (x, y) : \sum_{k=1}^{K} z_k x_{kn} \leqq x_n, \quad n = 1, \ldots, N \right.
$$

(4.1)

$$
\sum_{k=1}^{K} z_k y_{km} \geqq y_m, \quad m = 1, \ldots, M
$$

$$
\left. z_k \geqq 0, \quad k = 1, \ldots, K \right\}
$$

where the input and output inequalities are reversed, which models the differing monotonicities which we refer to as input and output disposability. For the directional distance function to be consistent with these monotonicity properties, the directional input vector should seek to reduce inputs whereas the directional output vector should seek to increase outputs. This is consistent with profit maximization where cost (wx) is minimized and revenue (py) is maximized. Thus the input direction g_x is chosen from $\Re_{-}^{N}$ and the output direction g_y from $\Re_{+}^{M}$. One may of course choose $g_x \in \Re_{+}^{N}$ and subtract it, which is equivalent to choosing $g_x \in \Re_{-}^{N}$ and adding it to the observed inputs. What is required is that the choice of directions be consistent with the monotonicities of the technology.

The directional technology distance function may be estimated using DEA as follows,

$$
\vec{D}_t(x^{k'}, y^{k'}; g_x, g_y) = \qquad \max \beta
$$

(4.2)

$$
s.t. \quad \sum_{k=1}^{K} z_k x_{kn} \leqq x_{k'n} - \beta g_{x_n}, \quad n = 1, \ldots, N
$$

$$
\sum_{k=1}^{K} z_k y_{km} \geqq y_{k'm} + \beta g_{y_m}, \quad m = 1, \ldots, M
$$

$$
z_k \geqq 0, \qquad k = 1, \ldots, K.
$$

The distance function projects DMU $k's$ input vector $(x^{k'}, y^{k'})$ onto the frontier of the technology T by scaling β along the directional vector $g = (-g_x, g_y)$ which has been added to the observed data point. The following Figure 4.1 illustrates.

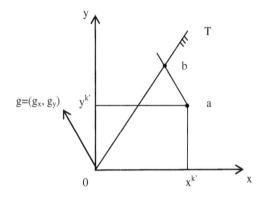

Fig. 4.1. Directional technology distance function.

The technology is given by T in the figure, where DMU k' is the point labeled 'a'. The distance function projects 'a' onto the frontier at 'b' in the direction $g = (g_x, g_y)$, where g_x is subtracted from $x_{k'n}$ and g_y is added to $y_{k'm}$. $\vec{D}_t(.)$ indicates that a DMU is efficient when $\vec{D}_t(.) = 0$ and inefficient when $\vec{D}_t(.) > 0$. Observations for which $\vec{D}_t(.) < 0$ are not feasible.

As an example, assume we have the following input output data:

$$\text{DMU 1} \quad \text{DMU 2}$$

$$
\begin{array}{ccc}
x & 1 & 1 \\
y & 1 & 2
\end{array}
\tag{4.3}
$$

These data give rise to two DEA problems. For DMU 2 we have the following DEA estimator

$$\max \beta_2 \tag{4.4}$$

$$s.t. \ z_1 1 + z_2 1 \leq 1 - \beta_2 g_x$$

$$z_1 1 + z_2 2 \geq 2 + \beta_2 g_y$$

$$z_1, z_2 \geq 0,$$

i.e.,

$$\beta_2 g_x \leqq 1 - z_1 - z_2$$
$$\beta_2 g_y \leqq z_1 + 2z_2 - 2 \tag{4.5}$$

or

$$\beta_2 \leqq \frac{z_2 - 1}{g_x + g_y}. \tag{4.6}$$

It follows that DMU 2 is efficient, independent of the direction chosen as long as it is non-negative. We see this by setting $z_1 = 0, z_2 = 1$, which yields $\beta_2 = 0$.

The DEA estimator for DMU 1 is

$$\max \beta_1 \tag{4.7}$$
$$s.t. \ z_1 1 + z_2 1 \leqq 1 - \beta_1 g_x$$
$$z_1 1 + z_2 1 \geqq 1 + \beta_1 g_y$$
$$z_1, z_2 \geqq 0,$$

which yields

$$\beta_1 \leqq \frac{1}{g_x + g_y} \tag{4.8}$$

as long as $(g_x + g_y)$ is nonnegative, $\beta_1 > 0$, thus DMU 1 is inefficient; it could increase its output and decrease its input simultaneously. Here we see that the inefficiency score does depend on the direction chosen. If we choose the direction vector as $(1, 1)$, which for DMU 1 is the value of the data as well, we would have $\beta_1 = 1/2$.

If we had chosen other directions, for example $g = (0, g_y)$ or $g = (g_x, 0)$, we obtain output and input directional distance functions, respectively. Suppose for example we choose $g = (x^{k'}, 0)$, then we have

$$\max \beta \tag{4.9}$$

$$s.t. \quad \sum_{k=1}^{K} z_k x_{kn} \leqq x_{k'n} - \beta x_{k'n}, \quad n = 1, \ldots, N$$

$$\sum_{k=1}^{K} z_k y_{km} \geqq y_{k'm}, \qquad m = 1, \ldots, M$$

$$z_k \geqq 0, \qquad\qquad k = 1, \ldots, K,$$

where the input constraints may be rewritten as

$$\sum_{k=1}^{K} z_k x_{kn} \leqq (1 - \beta) x_{k'n}, \quad n = 1, \ldots, N. \tag{4.10}$$

This is a version of Shephard's input distance function, otherwise familiar as the Farrell (1957) input oriented technical efficiency index, see the Appendix to Chapter 2.

4.2 Aggregation and Directional Vectors

In this section we investigate the choice of directional vectors when we are interested in aggregation of the resulting efficiency scores. To simplify our problem, including issues with allocative inefficiencies we assume that the DMU or firm produces a single output using a vector $x = (x_1, \ldots, x_N)$ of inputs. In this case we can define a production function as

$$F(x) = \max\{y : (x, y) \in T\}. \tag{4.11}$$

From our assumptions on T — closed with bounded output sets — the maximum exists and the production function is well-defined. The output set may now be defined in terms of the production function, i.e.,

$$P(x) = [0, F(x)]. \tag{4.12}$$

Let $g_y > 0$ be the direction vector — here a scalar — then the directional output distance function is given by

$$\begin{aligned}
\vec{D}_o(x, y; g_y) &= \sup\{\beta : (y + \beta g_y \in P(x)\} \quad\quad (4.13) \\
&= \sup\{\beta : (y + \beta g_y \in [0, F(x)]\} \\
&= \sup\{\beta : (y + \beta g_y \leqq F(x)\} \\
&= \frac{F(x) - y}{g_y}.
\end{aligned}$$

Next suppose that there are $k = 1, \ldots, K$ DMUs and define the maximal aggregate output of these DMUs as

$$\sum_{k-1}^{K} F^k(x^k) \quad\quad (4.14)$$

and aggregate observed output as

$$\sum_{k=1}^{K} y^k. \quad\quad (4.15)$$

The aggregate directional output distance function, with direction g_y^a is then

$$\begin{aligned}
\vec{D}_o\left(x^1, \ldots, x^K, \sum_{k=1}^{K} y^k; g_y^a\right) &= \sup\left\{\beta : \left(\sum_{k=1}^{K} y^k + \beta g_y^a\right)\right. \quad\quad (4.16) \\
&\left. \leqq \sum_{k=1}^{K} F^k(x^k)\right\} \\
&= \frac{\sum_{k=1}^{K} F^k(x^k) - \sum_{k=1}^{K} y^k}{g_y^a}.
\end{aligned}$$

This may well differ from

$$\sum_{k=1}^{K} \vec{D}_o^k(x^k, y^k; g_y^k) \quad\quad (4.17)$$

i.e., the sum of the individual firm directional output distance functions if $g_y^a \neq g_y^k$, i.e., if not all firms are projected in the same direction. If they do all face the same direction vector then we have

$$\vec{D}_o(x^1, \ldots, x^K, \sum_{k=1}^{K} y^k; g_y) = \frac{\sum_{k=1}^{K} F^k(x^k) - \sum_{k=1}^{K} y^k}{g_y} \quad (4.18)$$

$$= \sum_{k=1}^{K} \left(\frac{F^k(x^k) - y^k}{g_y} \right)$$

$$= \sum_{k=1}^{K} \vec{D}_o^k(x^k, y^k; g_y^k)$$

which is the case when aggregation is successful, since the aggregate (industry) distance function is equal to the sum of the individual firm distance functions.

Thus if we would like to sum individual scores to attain the aggregate score, we have learned that every firm should have the same direction vector. This result may be generalized to the case of multiple outputs.

Returning to our expression

$$\vec{D}_o(x, y; g_y) = \frac{F(x) - y}{g_y}, \quad (4.19)$$

we can see that for an inefficient DMU, its score depends on g_y. However, if we choose $g_y = 1$ we have

$$\vec{D}_o(x, y; 1) = F(x) - y, \quad (4.20)$$

which tells us that the inefficiency score is just the difference between maximal output $F(x)$ and observed output y, which is a strong argument for choosing $g_y = 1$. Again we can show that this generalizes to the multiple output case as well.

4.3 Endogenizing the Directional Vector

It may be the case that the researcher would like to estimate a directional distance function yet is inhibited by having to choose a direction vector; in that case there is an alternative which is to endogenize the direction vectors, thus making them a part of the optimization problem.[1] To understand how this works, we need to know onto which subset of the technology the optimization problem projects the DMU under evaluation. We consider three subsets of the technology, where we here represent the technology by its output sets $P(x), x \in \Re_+^N$.

We begin with the subset known as the isoquant, defined as

$$\text{Isoq } P(x) = \{y : y \in P(x), \lambda y \notin P(x), \lambda > 1\}. \qquad (4.21)$$

This definition is due to Shephard (1970), and differs from the standard textbook definition — usually defined on the input sets — which are in terms of local sets of functions. We illustrate the Shephard definition of the isoquant in the next figure.

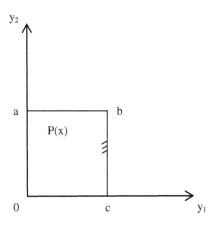

Fig. 4.2.   Isoq $P(x)$ and Eff $P(x)$.

The output set $P(x)$ is bounded by 0abc0, and the isoquant is the subset abc.

Recall from the Appendix to Chapter 2 that Shephard's output distance function is defined as

$$D_o(x, y) = \inf\{\lambda : y/\lambda \in P(x)\}. \qquad (4.22)$$

---

[1]This section builds on Färe, Grosskopf and Whittaker (in press).

From this definition we have the following **Indication Property**

$$D_o(x, y) = 1 \text{ if and only if } y \in \text{Isoq } P(x). \tag{4.23}$$

And since the Farrell (1957) output-oriented technical efficiency measure is frequently defined as the reciprocal of the output distance function, i.e.,

$$F_o(x, y) = 1/D_o(x, y), \tag{4.24}$$

we conclude that it has the **Indication Property**

$$F_o(x, y) = 1 \text{ if and only if } y \in \text{Isoq } P(x). \tag{4.25}$$

Another important part of the boundary of the output set is the efficient subset given by

$$\text{Eff } P(x) = \{y : y \in P(x), \hat{y} \notin P(x) \text{ if } \hat{y} \geq y, \hat{y} \neq y\}. \tag{4.26}$$

In Figure 4.2 this set consists of point b. Starting at point b, if we increase output in any of its components (here y_1 or y_2) without making any other smaller, the new output vector $\hat{y}$ will be outside of $P(x)$, thus by the definition point b is in the efficient subset of $P(x)$. Points in the efficient subset are also often referred to as Pareto-Koopmans efficient.

Note that since $P(x)$ is closed and bounded, Isoq $P(x)$ and Eff $P(x)$ are nonempty. Furthermore

$$\text{Eff } P(x) \subseteq \text{Isoq } P(x), \tag{4.27}$$

and as shown in the figure they need not coincide.

Next we turn to an efficiency measure which projects DMUs under evaluation to the efficient subset of $P(x)$ rather than to its isoquant. This measure, which we call the Russell measure was proposed by Färe and Lovell (1978). Thus the output-oriented Russell measure $R_o(x, y)$ has the following indication property

$$R_o(x, y) = 1 \text{ if and only if } y \in \text{Eff } P(x). \tag{4.28}$$

This measure is defined as

$$R_o(x, y) = \left\{ \frac{\lambda_1 + \dots, \lambda_M}{M} : (\lambda_1 y_1, \dots, \lambda_M y_M) \in P(x) \right\}, \qquad (4.29)$$

where we have assumed $y_m > 0, m = 1, \dots, M$.[2]

Returning to the directional distance function and its direction vector which we wish to endogenize, we make use of the slack-based directional distance function developed by Färe and Grosskopf (2010a,b).[3] Here we restrict our attention to the output oriented version, namely

$$\overrightarrow{SD}_o(x^{k'}, y^{k'}; 1, 1) = \max \beta_1 + \dots, \beta_M \qquad (4.30)$$

$$s.t. \quad \sum_{k=1}^{K} z_k x_{kn} \leqq x_{k'n}, \qquad n = 1, \dots, N$$

$$\sum_{k=1}^{K} z_k y_{km} \geqq y_{k'm} + \beta_m \cdot 1, \quad m = 1, \dots, M$$

$$z_k \geqq 0, \qquad k = 1, \dots, K$$

$$\beta_m \geqq 0, \qquad m = 1, \dots, M.$$

In contrast to the directional output distance function

$$\vec{D}_o(x^{k'}, y^{k'}; g_y) = \max \beta \qquad (4.31)$$

$$s.t. \quad \sum_{k=1}^{K} z_k x_{kn} \leqq x_{k'n}, \qquad n = 1, \dots, N$$

$$\sum_{k=1}^{K} z_k y_{km} \geqq y_{k'm} + \beta g_{y_m}, \quad m = 1, \dots, M$$

$$z_k \geqq 0, \qquad k = 1, \dots, K,$$

where we have a common β or scaling factor, the slack based measure has a different β_m for each type of output. Also the direction equals one for each

---

[2]This assumption may be relaxed.
[3]See Tone (2001) for another slack-based measure.

m in the slack based measure, rather than g_m for the directional distance function.

When $(x^{k'}, y^{k'})$ are efficient with respect to the directional output distance function, i.e., $\vec{D}_o(x^{k'}, y^{k'}; g_y) = 0$, then the indication is

$$\vec{D}_o(x^{k'}, y^{k'}; g_y) = 0 \text{ if and only if } y \in \text{g Isoq } P(x), \qquad (4.32)$$

where the g Isoq $P(x)$ is defined as

$$\text{g Isoq } P(x) = \{y : y \in P(x), y' \notin P(x) \text{ if } y' = y + \beta g_y, \quad \beta > 0\}. \qquad (4.33)$$

In contrast, the slack-based distance function has the following indication property

$$\vec{SD}_o(x, y; 1, 1) = 0 \text{ if and only if } y \in \text{ Eff } P(x). \qquad (4.34)$$

Thus the slack-based distance function, like the Russell measure, projects the output vector onto the efficient subset of $P(x)$. See the appendix for a proof.

One interesting feature of the slack-based distance function is that it allows some y_m to be zero.[4] To verify this property, take $y_M = 0$, then the associated output constraint becomes

$$\sum_{k=1}^{K} z_k y_{kM} \geq 0 + \beta_M \geq 0, \qquad (4.35)$$

where the last inequality holds since $\beta_m \geq 0, m = 1, \ldots, M$, thus given $z_M = 1, \beta_M = 0$, and $y_M = 0$, allows for the optimization problem to have a solution.

Next we endogenize the direction vectors by introducing them into the optimization problem. For this new problem to have a solution we need to assure that these endogenous directions are 'compact'. We do this by taking

$$\sum_{m=1}^{M} g_{y_m} = 1, \qquad (4.36)$$

---

[4]See the Kemeny, Morgenstern and Thompson (1956) conditions in Chapter 2.

and our new problem with endogenous gs is

$$\max_{z,\beta,g} \beta \tag{4.37}$$

$$s.t. \quad \sum_{k=1}^{K} z_k x_{kn} \leqq x_{k'n}, \qquad n = 1, \ldots, N$$

$$\sum_{k=1}^{K} z_k y_{km} \geqq y_{k'm} + \beta g_{y_m}, \quad m = 1, \ldots, M$$

$$z_k \geqq 0, \qquad k = 1, \ldots, K$$

$$\sum_{m=1}^{M} g_{y_m} = 1.$$

This problem, which is nonlinear, has β, z and the direction vector $g = (g_{y_1}, \ldots, g_{y_M})$ as variables. This estimator may be transformed into a linear maximization problem, which turns out to be our slack-based distance function estimator

$$\max_{\beta,z} \beta_1 + \ldots, \beta_M \tag{4.38}$$

$$s.t. \quad \sum_{k=1}^{K} z_k x_{kn} \leqq x_{k'n}, \qquad n = 1, \ldots, N$$

$$\sum_{k=1}^{K} z_k y_{km} \geqq y_{k'm} + \beta_m \cdot 1, \quad m = 1, \ldots, M$$

$$z_k \geqq 0, \qquad k = 1, \ldots, K$$

$$\beta_m \geqq 0, \qquad m = 1, \ldots, M$$

$$\sum_{m=1}^{M} g_{y_m} = 1.$$

To prove this let β_m^* be optimal, and take g such that

$$\beta_m^* = \beta g_{y_m}, \quad m = 1, \ldots, M \tag{4.39}$$

$$\sum_{m=1}^{M} g_{y_m} = 1,$$

and rewrite the slack-based problem as

$$\max \beta g_{y_1} + \cdots + \beta g_{y_M} \tag{4.40}$$

$$s.t. \quad \sum_{k=1}^{K} z_k x_{kn} \leqq x_{k'n}, \qquad n = 1, \ldots, N$$

$$\sum_{k=1}^{K} z_k y_{km} \geqq y_{k'm} + \beta g_{y_m}, \quad m = 1, \ldots, M$$

$$z_k \geqq 0, \qquad k = 1, \ldots, K$$

$$\beta_m \geqq 0, \qquad m = 1, \ldots, M$$

$$\sum_{m=1}^{M} g_{y_m} = 1.$$

This can be simplified to

$$\max \beta \tag{4.41}$$

$$s.t. \quad \sum_{k=1}^{K} z_k x_{kn} \leqq x_{k'n}, \qquad n = 1, \ldots, N$$

$$\sum_{k=1}^{K} z_k y_{km} \geqq y_{k'm} + \beta g_{y_m}, \quad m = 1, \ldots, M$$

$$z_k \geqq 0, \qquad k = 1, \ldots, K$$

$$\sum_{m=1}^{M} g_{y_m} = 1,$$

which is equivalent to our endogenous g problem. We can also show that the endogenous g problem may be transformed into the slack-based problem. To see this, multiply the objective in the endogenous g problem with $(\sum_{m=1}^{M} g_{y_m} = 1)$ and set

$$\beta_m = \beta g_{y_m} \cdot 1, \quad m = 1, \ldots, M, \tag{4.42}$$

then the slack-based problem follows.

Next we show how we may use the slack-based directional distance function problem to determine the g vector. We consider three cases:

(i) all $\beta_m = 0, m = 1, \ldots, M$
(ii) all $\beta_m > 0, m = 1, \ldots, M$
(iii) at least one $\beta_m = 0$, the others strictly positive.

If all $\beta_m = 0$ then the DMU is efficient and we may arbitrarily set

$$\beta_m = 1/M \text{ for all } m. \tag{4.43}$$

If all $\beta_m > 0$, we consider the case of M $= 3$, then we have

$$\beta = \frac{\beta_1}{g_1} = \frac{\beta_2}{g_2} = \frac{\beta_3}{g_3}, \tag{4.44}$$

where we have taken $g_m = g_{y_m}$ for notational convenience. The above together with

$$g_1 + g_2 + g_3 = 1 \tag{4.45}$$

yields

$$\frac{g_1}{g_3} + \frac{g_2}{g_3} + 1 = \frac{1}{g_3} \tag{4.46}$$

and

$$\frac{\beta_1}{\beta_3} = \frac{g_1}{g_3} \tag{4.47}$$

thus

$$\frac{\beta_1}{\beta_3} + \frac{\beta_2}{\beta_3} + 1 = \frac{1}{g_3} \tag{4.48}$$

and

$$g_3 = \frac{\beta_3}{\beta_1 + \beta_2 + \beta_3}. \tag{4.49}$$

The same applies for g_2 and g_2. Thus the $g's$ are the shares of the scores, $\beta_m, m = 1, 2, 3$.

In the third case we set the g_m for the DMU with $\beta_m = 0$ to be zero, and then we have again that the remaining $g's$ as shares of the $\beta's$.

Finally we give an example with the simple artificial data set seen below.[5]

DMU	1	2
y_1	1	2
y_2	1	2
x	1	1

From this data, the slack based solution for DMU 1 is

$$\beta_1^* = \beta_2^* = 1. \tag{4.50}$$

Thus the $g's$ for DMU 1 are

$$g_m = \frac{1}{1+1} = 1/2, \quad m = 1, 2. \tag{4.51}$$

For DMU 2 we have

$$\beta_1^* = \beta_2^* = 0 \tag{4.52}$$

and we may set

$$g_1 = g_2 = 1/2. \tag{4.53}$$

4.4 Appendix

Theorem: $\overrightarrow{SD}(x, y; 1, 1) = 0 \Leftrightarrow y \in \text{Eff } P(x)$.

Proof: Assume $y \notin \text{Eff } P(x)$, then there exists a feasible $y' \in P(x)$, $y' \geq y$, $y' \neq y$ i.e., y' is larger than y in at least one coordinate, hence β_m in that coordinate can take a positive value. Hence $\overrightarrow{SD}(x, y; 1, 1) > 0$, showing that $\overrightarrow{SD}(x, y; 1, 1) = 0 \Rightarrow y \in \text{Eff } P(x)$.

To show the converse, assume $y \in \text{Eff } P(x)$. Since $\beta_m \geq 0$, none can be positive, hence $\overrightarrow{SD}(x, y; 1, 1) = 0$. **Q.E.D.**

---

[5]This example is borrowed from Färe, Grosskopf and Whittaker (2013).

Chapter 5

DEA and Time Substitution

This chapter addresses a single DEA topic, time substitution. This topic is the study of how to allocate resources in time, with the two options (i) determine when to apply inputs and (ii) how long, i.e., in how many periods should inputs be used. These options allow the decision maker to determine when to start production and for how long to produce. The topic was initiated by Shephard and Färe (1980) in connection with ship building, refined by Färe and Grosskopf (1996), and finally given a DEA formulation by Färe, Grosskopf, and Margaritis (2010). Their results are presented and generalized here.

After an introductory theoretical presentation we devote the rest of the chapter to an empirical application examining the Pact for Stability and Growth adopted by the countries comprising the single currency Euro zone.

5.1 Theoretical Underpinning

The idea of time substitution was discussed by Shephard and Färe (1980) and deals with the idea "when should inputs be used." A producer may wait and at the end work with high intensity or go about life evenly. The problem of time substitution has been discussed by Färe and Grosskopf (1996) and Färe, Grosskopf, and Margaritis (2010). Here we build on their theoretical work. In the next section we apply the theory to two problems: when should inputs be used and government purchases made to produce GDP given a government debt constraint, and, when should inputs be used and government purchases made in order to minimize the buildup of government debt given a target level of real GDP growth?

To set the stage let technology be

$$T = \{(x, y) : x \text{ can produce } y\}$$

with $x = (x_1, \ldots, x_N)$ a vector of inputs and y a scalar output. Define the production function as

$$F(x) = \max\{y : (x, y) \in T\}.$$

By our standard assumptions on T, this function exists and it is a representation of the technology, i.e.,

$$(x, y) \in T \text{ if and only if } F(x) \geqq y.$$

Time substitution models the various ways inputs can be applied to production. To illustrate, consider Figure 5.1.

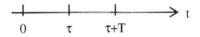

$$0 \qquad \tau \qquad \tau{+}T$$

Fig. 5.1.   Timeline of input use.

Assume that inputs are non-negative vectors which can be allocated over our timeline. In addition, we assume that inputs are essential for production, i.e.,

$$F(0) = 0, \tag{5.1}$$

which implies that if there is no input there is no output — no free lunch. Next suppose that the total amount of inputs will be used over the time interval $[\tau, \tau + \Gamma]$, so that

$$\begin{aligned} F(x^t) &= 0, \quad 0 \leqq t < \tau \\ F(x^t) &> 0, \quad \tau \leqq t \leqq \tau + \Gamma \\ F(x^t) &= 0, \quad \tau + \Gamma \leqq t. \end{aligned} \tag{5.2}$$

This means that production is positive only on the 'support of inputs', i.e., when inputs are applied to production. In this framework there are two ways in which input use may be changed:

(i) change τ
(ii) change Γ.

In the first case if τ is increased input use is delayed — the initial application of inputs is postponed, keeping the same length of the production period Γ. In the second case the length of the production period is changed: a smaller Γ yields higher input intensity, whereas a larger Γ implies more 'leisurely' production.

The time substitution problem is to find the 'best' τ and Γ given some objective function. Since data are generally reported in discrete time rather than continuously,[1] we think of the timeline as discrete intervals, so that x^t means the amount of inputs applied in period t, which may be a week, month or year, for example.

Our first problem is to find the best τ and Γ when total production, in this case a scalar, is maximized:

$$\max \sum_{t=0}^{\infty} F^t(x^t), \, x^\tau + \cdots + x^{\tau+\Gamma} \leq \overline{x}, \tag{5.3}$$

where $\overline{x}$ is a finite amount of inputs and τ and Γ are given. Let $F^t(x^t)$ be continuous and $F^t(x^t) = 0$ for $t \notin [\tau, \tau + \Gamma]$. Then a solution exists to our maximization problem. Denote the solution by $F(\tau, \Gamma, \overline{x})$ and our time substitution problem is to find

$$\max_{\tau, \Gamma} F(\tau, \Gamma, \overline{x}). \tag{5.4}$$

To provide intuition about the time substitution model we follow Färe, Grosskopf, and Margaritis (2010) and look at its solution under two economic scenarios: (i) returns to scale and (ii) technical change.

In case one, suppose there are two periods τ and Γ and that the single input $\overline{x}$ is allocated over these periods; i.e.,

$$x^\tau + x^{\tau+\Gamma} \leq \overline{x}. \tag{5.5}$$

We assume that there is no technical change and that the production function is

$$F(x) = x^\alpha. \tag{5.6}$$

---

[1] As scanner data becomes more frequently available, it can more closely approximate continuous time.

If $\alpha > 1$ we have increasing returns to scale, and constant or decreasing returns to scale if $\alpha = 1$ or $\alpha < 1$, respectively. Our maximization problem is

$$\max (x^{\tau})^{\alpha} + (x^{\tau+\Gamma})^{\alpha} \text{ s.t. } x^{\tau} + x^{\tau+\Gamma} \leqq \bar{x}. \qquad (5.7)$$

The solutions to this problem are

$$\begin{aligned}
\alpha > 1 \quad &(i) \ x^{\tau} = 0 \quad \text{and} \quad x^{\tau+\Gamma} = \bar{x} \\
&(ii) \ x^{\tau} = \bar{x} \quad \text{and} \quad x^{\tau+\Gamma} = 0
\end{aligned} \qquad (5.8)$$

$$\begin{aligned}
\alpha = 1 \quad &(iii) \ x^{\tau} + x^{\tau+\Gamma} = \bar{x} \\
\alpha < 1 \quad &(iv) \ x^{\tau} = x^{\tau+\Gamma} = \bar{x}.
\end{aligned}$$

In words, under increasing returns to scale, use all of the inputs at one time, but the time does not matter; the decision maker should take advantage of increasing returns to scale. When $\alpha = 1$ (CRS) the decision maker is indifferent as to when to use input and finally, under decreasing returns to scale inputs are split equally between the two periods. Thus, in all three cases the solution is independent of τ and Γ.

Our second example is the case of technical change under constant returns to scale. Again assume there are two periods τ and Γ. We assume the production function is of the form

$$F^t(x^t) = A(t) \cdot x^t, \qquad (5.9)$$

where $A(t)$ is the technical change factor. Our problem is now to

$$\max A(\tau) \cdot x^{\tau} + A(\tau + \Gamma) \cdot x^{\tau+\Gamma} \text{ s.t. } x^{\tau} + x^{\tau+\Gamma} \leqq \bar{x}. \qquad (5.10)$$

If there is technical progress, i.e.,

$$t' > t \Rightarrow A(t') > A(t), \qquad (5.11)$$

then by increasing the length of the production period from Γ to Γ', and allocating all $\bar{x}$ to the latter period we have

$$A(\tau) \cdot 0 + A(\tau + \Gamma) \cdot \bar{x} < A(\tau) \cdot 0 + A(\tau + \Gamma') \cdot \bar{x}, \qquad (5.12)$$

and the solution tells us to extend the support from $[\tau, \tau + \Gamma]$ to $[\tau, \tau + \Gamma']$.

In the case of technical regress, i.e.,

$$t' > t \Rightarrow A(t') < A(t), \tag{5.13}$$

it follows that the production should be done early, i.e.,

$$A(\tau) \cdot \bar{x}, \text{ where } x^{\tau} = \bar{x} \text{ and } x^{\tau+\Gamma} = 0. \tag{5.14}$$

Similarly if there is technical progress it pays to delay the production by increasing τ and if there is technical regress it pays to begin production earlier by decreasing τ. We conclude that technical change impacts choice of τ and Γ, but returns to scale does not.

Given that we have finite τ and Γ, the DEA solution to the time substitution problem is obtained by solving

$$\max \quad y^{\tau} + \cdots + y^{\tau+\Gamma} \tag{5.15}$$

$$\text{s.t.} \quad y^{\tau} \leqq \sum_{k=1}^{K} z_k^{\tau} y_k^{\tau}$$

$$\sum_{k=1}^{K} z_k^{\tau} x_k^{\tau} \leqq x_n^{\tau}, \qquad n = 1, \ldots, N$$

$$z_k^{\tau} \geqq 0, \qquad k = 1, \ldots, K$$

$$\vdots$$

$$y^{\tau+\Gamma} \leqq \sum_{k=1}^{K} z_k^{\tau+\Gamma} y_k^{\tau+\Gamma}$$

$$\sum_{k=1}^{K} z_k^{\tau+\Gamma} x_k^{\tau+\Gamma} \leqq x_n^{\tau+\Gamma}, \qquad n = 1, \ldots, N$$

$$z_k^{\tau+\Gamma} \geqq 0, \qquad k = 1, \ldots, K$$

$$x_{kn}^{\tau} + \cdots + x_{kn}^{\tau+\Gamma} \leqq \bar{x}_n \qquad n = 1, \ldots, N$$

where the last inequality sums the allocation of inputs over the production period. For each DMU, $\bar{x}_{nk'}$ is given and the problem is solved for each τ and Γ within the time period. Thus, for example if we have $t = 0, 1, 2$, we solve for

τ	Γ
0	0, 1, 2
1	0, 1
2	0

For instance, when $\tau = 0$ and $\Gamma = 0$ production begins and ends in period $t = 0$. When $\tau = 0$ and $\Gamma = 1$, production begins in period 0 and ends in $t = 1$. If $\tau = 0$ and $\Gamma = 2$ then production begins in $t = 0$ and ends in $t = 2$. The maximum over all of these solutions gives the optimal τ and Γ for the particular DMU.

A generalization of the above problem is to identify inputs that are fixed in time and inputs which can be allocated over time, e.g., labor may be allocated over time, while capital may not. In this case we reformulate the input constraints — we illustrate here just for τ — other periods are similar.

$$\sum_{k=1}^{K} z_k^\tau x_{kn}^\tau \leqq x_{k'n}^\tau, \quad n = 1, \dots, N'$$

$$\sum_{k=1}^{K} z_k^\tau x_{kn}^\tau \leqq \overline{x}_{k'n}^\tau, \quad n = N' + 1, \dots, N. \tag{5.16}$$

The summing up constraints then apply only to the $n = N' + 1, \dots, N$ inputs.

Assume next that $y \in \Re_+^M$ and that we know the output prices $p \in \Re_+^M$. In this case there is a simple generalization of the time substitution problem to multiple outputs. Note that revenue equals

$$p_1 y_1 + \cdots + p_M y_M. \tag{5.17}$$

If each DMU faces the same prices, we can solve the revenue maximization problem as a DEA time substitution problem

$$\max \ p^\tau y^\tau + \cdots + p^{\tau+\Gamma} y^{\tau+\Gamma} \tag{5.18}$$

$$s.t. \quad y_m^\tau \leqq \sum_{k=1}^{K} z_k^\tau y_k^\tau \qquad m = 1, \dots, M$$

$$\sum_{k=1}^{K} z_k^\tau x_k^\tau \leq x_n^\tau, \qquad n = 1, \dots, N$$

$$z_k^\tau \geq 0, \qquad k = 1, \dots, K$$

$$\vdots$$

$$y_m^{\tau+\Gamma} \leq \sum_{k=1}^{K} z_k^{\tau+\Gamma} y_k^{\tau+\Gamma}$$

$$\sum_{k=1}^{K} z_k^{\tau+\Gamma} x_k^{\tau+\Gamma} \leq x_n^{\tau+\Gamma}, \qquad n = 1, \dots, N$$

$$z_k^{\tau+\Gamma} \geq 0, \qquad k = 1, \dots, K$$

$$x_{kn}^\tau + \cdots + x_{kn}^{\tau+\Gamma} \leq \bar{x}_n \qquad n = 1, \dots, N.$$

Note that prices may differ across periods even when DMUs face the same prices within those periods.

5.2 Reassessing the EU Stability and Growth Pact

(by Färe, R., Grosskopf, S., Margaritis, D. and Weber, W.L.)

Monetary union among sovereign countries helps facilitate trade by reducing transaction costs of currency exchange. When countries have different levels of sovereign default risk, an agreement among those countries to form a monetary union can lend a deficit bias to the area as a whole as interest rate differences between those countries disappear (Schuknecht, 2002). A deficit bias can also occur when an aging population defers payment for retirement and health care to future generations, when fiscal policy is captured by special interests, or when lower level governments think they will receive transfers from a central government in the event of insolvency. To alleviate the bias toward deficits, member countries can agree to a fiscal constitution requiring, for instance, balanced government budgets except in emergencies and/or maximum allowable ratios of government debt to GDP. However, rules can be time inconsistent, since there may be instances when it is sub-optimal to abide by previous commitments.

The 1992 Maastricht Treaty proposed a monetary union among European countries that met certain fiscal criteria. From 1992 to 1998 the fiscal deficits of the European countries considering monetary union improved from an average of 5% of GDP to only 2% of GDP. However, only Ireland, Luxembourg, and Finland met the balanced budget requirement. Although France and Germany were producing near potential output in 1998 they continued to run deficits in excess of 2% of GDP (Schuknecht *et al.*, 2011). In 1998, eleven European countries formed the initial euro currency zone and the euro came into existence. Subsequently, Greece was admitted into the euro zone in 2001, followed by Slovenia (2007), Malta and Cyprus (2008), Slovakia (2009), and Estonia (2011) bringing the total number of euro zone countries to seventeen. As part of the 1992 Maastricht Treaty member countries agreed to a "no-bailout" rule prohibiting the European Central Bank from directly acquiring the sovereign debt of member countries and holding harmless member countries for the debts of another country.

To formalize the budget criteria under the Maastricht Treaty the 1998 Pact for Stability and Growth required that the budgets of member countries be balanced or in surplus during normal times, so that automatic fiscal stabilizers could be allowed to operate. Allowable exemptions include countries which have experienced 2% declines in GDP. Those countries having excessive deficits would be required to contribute 0.2% of GDP to a non-interest bearing deposit at the European Central Bank that would convert to a fine that could rise to as much of 0.5% of GDP given agreement by a majority of countries (Schuknecht *et al.*, 2011).

One of the main rationales behind formal fiscal rules, such as the Pact for Stability and Growth, is that the deficit bias that arises from the common pool problem among member countries could create contagion effects if default in one country spills over to other countries. To test for contagion effects Eichengreen and Wyplosz (1998) examine US states and find little evidence of interstate contagion effects. In addition, they test the null hypothesis of no interest rate spillovers between European countries using Granger causality tests. They conclude that European countries borrow on a global capital market with only small interest rate spillovers between countries. Furthermore, Eichengreen and Wyplosz (1998) simulate the effects of Stability Pact rules for OECD countries and find that the gap between potential and actual GDP increases as the budget surplus increases.

Since the Stability Pact rules weaken sovereign fiscal authority, the rules undermine citizen support for market reforms, especially policies that make labor markets more flexible and open.

Wyplosz (2012) defines fiscal discipline as occurring when the long-run debt to GDP ratio is stationary. Using an augmented Dickey-Fuller test and the KPSS stationary test he finds evidence of a non-stationary debt to GDP ratio for 15 out of 19 OECD countries during 1960–2011. It is important for fiscal rules to be flexible enough to accommodate unforeseen emergencies such as the bursting of housing or stock market bubbles or a financial crisis. However, the temptation to amend a fiscal rule becomes greatest when it is needed most: at the point the rule becomes binding (Wyplosz, 2012). The success of Ulysses in hearing the sirens sing was only possible because his faithful crew followed his orders. Will today's European Monetary Union odyssey become a Greek tragedy because fiscal rules were not followed? Or, as austerity opponents argue, were the rules the source of instability contributing to the on-going debt crisis in countries such as Greece?

In this section we simulate the effects of the Pact for Stability and Growth by examining the lost output that might result from budget rules that constrain the ratio of debt to GDP to be less than some arbitrary target. Rather than require that budgets meet the target in each and every year we impose a budget target over a longer period. Our method follows Färe, Grosskopf, and Margaritis (2010) and Färe *et al.* (2012) by allowing inputs to be substituted across time and governments to choose when to spend in order to maximize the sum of real GDP over time given the fiscal budget constraint. We also simulate how resources might be substituted across time in order to minimize government debt given a real GDP growth constraint.

5.3   Method

We consider two time substitution problems. The amount of capital and labor are fixed over the entire period but can be reallocated between periods. In the first problem budget deficits over the period 1995–2011 are balanced, but deficits in a given period are allowed if offset by a surplus in a different period. In the second problem we simulate a setting where countries attempt to minimize the sum of the budget deficits during the period subject to technological constraints and a policy goal of achieving 2% annual growth in real GDP throughout the period. In both problems the amount of labor and amount of capital are fixed over the entire period but labor and capital can be reallocated between periods.

We assume there are $k = 1, \ldots, K$ countries producing in $t = 1, \ldots, T$ periods. Each country is observed to produce y_k^t units of real GDP using L_k^t units of labor and K_k^t units of capital. Real GDP consists of the sum of real consumption expenditures, real investment expenditures, real government spending, and real net exports. The sum of consumption, investment, and net exports is represented by CIX_k^t and government spending equals G_k^t so that $y_k^t = CIX_k^t + G_k^t$. Government tax revenues, R_k^t, equal the product of the average tax rate, tr_k^t, and real GDP, $y_k^t : R_k^t = tr_k^t \times y_k^t$. The total amount of capital used during the period is represented by $\overline{K}_k = \sum_{t=1}^{T} K_k^t$ and the total labor used over the period is $\overline{L}_k = \sum_{t=1}^{T} L_k^t$. Transfer payments are represented by TP_k^t and the budget deficit is $deficit_k^t = G_k^t + TP_k^t - R_k^t$. The problem of time substitution involves choosing a period to begin production, τ and a length of time to engage in production, Γ so as to maximize production or minimize government debt.

For country o, the first problem takes the form:

$$\max_{z,G,K,L,\tau,\Gamma} \sum_{t=\tau}^{\tau+\Gamma} y^t = CIX_o^t + G^t \text{ subject to} \qquad (5.19)$$

$$L^t \geq \sum_{k=1}^{K} z_k^t L_k^t, \quad t = \tau, \ldots, \tau + \Gamma,$$

$$\sum_{t=\tau}^{\tau+\Gamma} L^t \leq \overline{L}_o$$

$$K^t \geq \sum_{k=1}^{K} z_k^t K_k^t, \quad t = \tau, \ldots, \tau + \Gamma,$$

$$\sum_{t=\tau}^{\tau+\Gamma} K^t \leq \overline{K}_o$$

$$CIX_o^t \leq \sum_{k=1}^{K} CIX_k^t, \quad t = \tau, \ldots, \tau + \Gamma,$$

$$G^t \leq \sum_{k=1}^{K} G_k^t, \quad t = \tau, \ldots, \tau + \Gamma,$$

$$R^t = tr_o^t \times \left(CIX_o^t + G^t\right), \qquad t = \tau, \ldots, \tau + \Gamma,$$

$$DEBT_{target} \geqq \sum_{t=\tau}^{\tau+\Gamma} \left(G^t + TP_o^t - R^t\right),$$

$$z_k^t \geqq 0, \quad t = \tau, \ldots, \tau + \Gamma, \quad k = 1, \ldots, K,$$

$$G^t \geqq 0, \quad K^t \geqq 0, \qquad t = \tau, \ldots, \tau + \Gamma.$$

In (5.19) the choice variables are the intensity variables, z_k^t, when to begin production, τ, the length of period to engage in production, Γ, the amount of labor and capital to be used in each period, L^t, K^t, and the amount of government spending, G^t. The optimal values determine government revenues, R^t. The $DEBT_{target}$ is a pre-determined value for the total accumulation of debt over the period. A debt target equal to zero would require government to run a balanced budget during the entire period but would allow a deficit in one year to be offset by a surplus in another year. Alternatively, the debt target could be set as a percent of GDP, such as a 2% target.

Given the difficulties of countries in the EU to obtain budget balance we consider an alternative problem. Here we simulate an objective whereby countries minimize the amount of debt they accumulate throughout the period subject to a constraint that requires a minimum amount of average annual real GDP growth. Real GDP in period $t = 1$ for country o is represented by y_o^1. Given the seventeen year period 1995–2011, let the sum of real GDP that satisfies the growth target be $\overline{y}_o = y_o^1 \times \sum_{t=0}^{16}(1+r)^t$, where r is the target for average annual real GDP growth. The second problem we consider takes the form:

$$\min_{z,G,K,L} \sum_{t=\tau}^{\tau+\Gamma}(G^t + TP_o^t - R^t) \text{ subject to} \qquad (5.20)$$

$$L^t \geqq \sum_{k=1}^{K} z_k^t L_k^t, \quad t = \tau, \ldots, \tau + \Gamma,$$

$$\sum_{t=\tau}^{\tau+\Gamma} L^t \leqq \overline{L}_o$$

$$K^t \geqq \sum_{k=1}^{K} z_k^t K_k^t, \quad t = \tau, \ldots, \tau + \Gamma,$$

$$\sum_{t=\tau}^{\tau+\Gamma} K^t \leqq \overline{K}_o$$

$$CIX_o^t \leqq \sum_{k=1}^{K} z_k^t CIX_k^t, \qquad t = \tau, \dots, \tau + \Gamma,$$

$$G^t \leqq \sum_{k=1}^{K} z_k^t G_k^t, \qquad t = \tau, \dots, \tau + \Gamma,$$

$$R^t = tr_o^t \times \left(CIX_o^t + G^t \right), \qquad t = \tau, \dots, \tau + \Gamma,$$

$$\sum_{t=\tau}^{\tau+\Gamma} \left(CIX_o^t + G^t \right) \geqq \overline{y}_o,$$

$$z_k^t \geqq 0, \quad t = \tau, \dots, \tau + \Gamma, \quad k = 1, \dots, K,$$

$$G^t \geqq 0, \quad K^t \geqq 0, \qquad t = \tau, \dots, \tau + \Gamma.$$

The choice variables for (5.20) are the same as problem (5.19): the intensity variables, z_k^t, when to begin production, τ, the length of period to engage in production, Γ, the amount of labor and capital to be used in each period, and the amount of government spending, G^t. However, in (5.20), countries are allowed to run deficits as long as the sum of real GDP throughout the period meets the target:

$$\sum_{t=\tau}^{\tau+\Gamma} \left(CIX_o^t + G^t \right) \geqq \overline{y}_o.$$

To estimate the time substitution model we employ panel data on 23 countries for the period 1995 to 2011. Included are the seventeen Euro zone countries plus Denmark, Japan, Sweden, Switzerland, the UK, and US. The six non-Euro zone countries are included since they help form the reference technology or because they are part of the European community. Table 5.1 reports descriptive statistics for the variables comprising problems (1) and (2) for the panel and for the seventeen Euro zone countries and six non-Euro zone countries. The average deficit to real GDP ratio equals 0.27 for the entire panel, with an average of 0.28 among the Euro zone countries and 0.22 for the six non-Euro zone countries. Finland had the smallest deficit to GDP ratio (largest surplus) of -0.068 in 2000 and in fact, ran a surplus from 1998 to 2008. Ireland had the largest deficit to GDP

Table 5.1. Descriptive statistics, 23 countries 1995–2011.

Variable	N	Mean	Std. Dev.	Minimum	Maximum
Labor = L	391	16650.2	30473.0	141.8	148295.0
Capital = K	391	2762.4	4991.8	6.0	26326.4
Y = CIX + G	391	952.1	1912.7	3.0	11173.2
CIX	391	780.2	1605.7	2.5	9521.7
Government expenditures = G + TP	391	397.2	721.7	1.2	3907.9
Government purchases = G	391	171.9	310.3	0.6	1662.0
Transfer payments = TP	391	225.2	412.5	0.6	2256.4
Tax revenue = R	391	361.1	646.4	1.1	3847.4
Average tax rate = tr	391	0.425	0.071	0.305	0.597
Deficit/Y	391	0.027	0.039	−0.068	0.313
17 Euro countries					
Labor = L	289	8222.7	11015.4	141.8	41028.4
Capital = K	289	1376.2	1956.4	6.0	7180.8
Y = CIX + G	289	412.6	597.5	3.0	2310.7
CIX	289	328.1	476.2	2.5	1865.6
Government expenditures = G + TP	289	199.9	294.4	1.2	1075.4
Government purchases = G	289	84.6	122.7	0.6	450.0
Transfer payments = TP	289	115.4	172.5	0.6	691.6
Tax revenue = R	289	187.3	275.5	1.1	1025.2
Average tax rate = tr	289	0.428	0.056	0.314	0.565
Deficit/Y	289	0.028	0.039	−0.068	0.313
6 Non-Euro countries (Denmark, Japan, Sweden, Switzerland, UK, US)					
Labor = L	110	40527.9	49605.4	2643.0	148295.0
Capital = K	110	6690.2	8014.1	392.9	26326.4
Y = CIX + G	110	2480.6	3149.0	153.4	11173.2
CIX	110	2061.1	2658.4	114.7	9521.7
Government expenditures = G + TP	110	956.0	1156.3	84.7	3907.9
Government purchases = G	110	419.5	495.1	27.9	1662.0
Transfer payments = TP	110	536.5	663.1	48.3	2256.4
Tax revenue = R	110	853.8	1032.3	77.9	3847.4
Average tax rate = tr	110	0.420	0.103	0.305	0.597
Deficit/Y	110	0.022	0.039	−0.050	0.115

Source: European Commission. Economic and Financial Affairs. Annual Macroeconomic Database. http://ec.europa.eu/economy_finance/db_indicators/ameco/zipped_en.htm.

ratio of 0.313 in 2010, but actually managed a surplus in eleven out of the seventeen years. Nine countries (Austria, France, Greece, Italy, Japan, Malta, Portugal, Slovakia, and Slovenia) ran deficits in every year 1995 to 2011. Luxembourg ran a deficit in only four years, followed by Finland with

Table 5.2.   Lost output due to the deficit target.

Country	Lost output given 0% deficit target	Lost output given 1% deficit target	Lost output given 2% deficit target	Lost output given 3% deficit target
Austria	0.202	0.176	0.152	0.130
Belgium	0.102	0.080	0.060	0.040
Cyprus	0.135	0.115	0.097	0.080
Estonia	0.093	0.076	0.060	0.045
Finland	0.027	0.008	0.000	0.000
France	0.176	0.151	0.127	0.104
Germany	0.188	0.166	0.144	0.124
Greece	0.447	0.419	0.391	0.365
Ireland	0.198	0.178	0.159	0.141
Italy	0.233	0.209	0.186	0.164
Japan	0.222	0.201	0.182	0.163
Luxembourg	0.000	0.000	0.000	0.000
Malta	0.097	0.078	0.060	0.043
Netherlands	0.116	0.095	0.075	0.056
Portugal	0.221	0.198	0.177	0.156
Slovakia	0.130	0.111	0.094	0.077
Slovenia	0.134	0.113	0.093	0.074
Spain	0.315	0.292	0.270	0.248
Denmark	0.000	0.000	0.000	0.000
Switzerland	0.034	0.018	0.005	0.000
Sweden	0.164	0.146	0.129	0.112
UK	0.159	0.139	0.120	0.101
US	0.154	0.136	0.118	0.101

$$\text{Lost output} = \left(\sum_{t=\tau}^{\tau+T} y_t^* (\text{No DEBT}_{target}) \bigg/ \sum_{t=1995}^{2011} y_t^* (\text{given DEBT}_{target}) \right) - 1$$

under constant returns to scale.

six years of deficits, and then Ireland, Estonia, and Switzerland with seven years of deficits.

In Table 5.2 (see also Figure 5.2) we report the results from solving problem (1) with a balanced budget and with debt (deficit) targets equal to 0%, 1%, 2%, and 3% of accumulated real GDP. As part of the solution to (1), the period to begin production was $\tau = 1995$ and the length of production was $\Gamma = 17$ years for all countries. To estimate the effects of the deficit constraint on real GDP we estimated (1) with and without the constraint $\text{DEBT}_{target} \geqq \sum_{t=\tau}^{\tau+\Gamma} (G^t + TP_o^t - R^t)$. The lost output due to the deficit constraint was calculated as

$$\text{Lost Output} = \left(\sum_{t=\tau}^{\tau+\Gamma} y_t^* (No\ \text{DEBT}_{target}) \Bigg/ \sum_{t=1995}^{2011} y_t^* (With\ \text{DEBT}_{target}) \right) - 1.$$

$$(5.21)$$

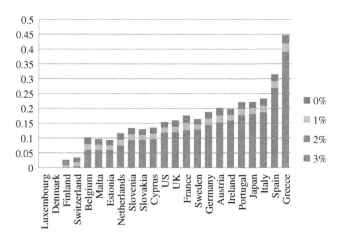

Fig. 5.2.   Lost output due to deficit target.

Luxembourg and Denmark experience no lost output given all four debt targets. For the 2% and 3% targets Finland would have experienced no lost output and for the 3% target Switzerland would have experienced no lost output. Such a result was expected since each of those countries had average deficit to real GDP ratios less than 0 during the period indicating that on average, the countries ran a surplus. Estonia also ran a cumulative surplus during the period but would have experienced some lost output. This result occurred because Estonia was inefficient and problem (1) maximizes potential real GDP = CIX + G by choosing G. For Estonia, the optimal level of government purchases (G) with no debt constraint was greater than the optimal level of government purchases with the debt constraint and the actual level of government purchases, which resulted in the lost potential output. Among the Euro zone countries the effect of the alternative debt constraints was greatest for Greece, followed by Spain. These countries would have suffered 45% and 31% in lost output had they balanced their

Table 5.3.   Actual debt and simulated debt given a growth target and time substitution.

Country	Actual average annual growth rate of real GDP	Actual debt accumulated (1995–2011) as a % of 2011 GDP	Simulated debt accumulated (1995–2011) given real GDP growth target
Austria	0.0193	0.375	0.314
Belgium	0.0165	0.276	0.240
Cyprus	0.0358	0.448	0.342
Estonia	0.0585	−0.046	−0.145
Finland	0.0310	−0.205	−0.246
France	0.0195	0.580	0.555
Germany	0.0090	0.417	0.370
Greece	0.0210	1.180	1.081
Ireland	0.0697	0.493	0.420
Italy	0.0239	0.592	0.533
Japan	0.0042	0.879	0.819
Luxembourg	0.0402	−0.247	−0.247
Malta	0.0376	0.769	0.758
Netherlands	0.0220	0.279	0.236
Portugal	0.0225	0.755	0.659
Slovakia	0.0519	0.566	0.512
Slovenia	−0.0030	0.509	0.483
Spain	0.0315	0.428	0.342
Denmark	0.0172	−0.103	−0.103
Switzerland	0.0198	−0.044	−0.129
Sweden	0.0307	0.040	0.029
UK	0.0458	0.623	0.558
US	0.0420	0.639	0.600

budgets during the period and even under a 3% debt target the two countries would have experienced 36.5% and 24.8% in lost output.

Among the non-Euro zone countries Japan would have experienced 23.3% lost output had they satisfied the 0% debt constraint with lost output falling to 16.3% for the 3% debt target. For the 3% target, Sweden, the UK and the US would have experienced approximately 11% lost output. For all countries (except those with 0% lost output), as the debt constraint is relaxed the lost output due to the constraint declines. For instance, relaxing the debt target from 2% to 3% resulted in an output gain for Greece equal to $(.391 - .365) \times 100\% = 2.6\%$.

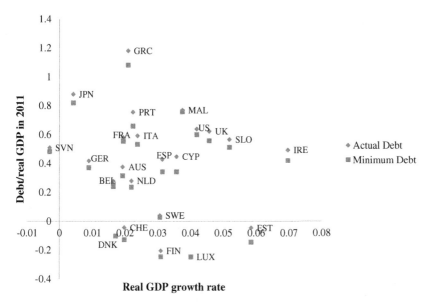

Fig. 5.3. Real GDP growth and Debt/real GDP in 2011.

Given the high cost in terms of lost output that most countries would incur from balancing their budgets we also estimated our second problem to determine the minimum potential debt that would be incurred if countries produced efficiently and achieved a given growth rate in real GDP. Table 5.3 (see also Figure 5.3) displays the actual average growth rate of real GDP for each of the countries.[2] During the 1995–2011 period Ireland had the highest average growth rate at 7% followed by Estonia, Slovakia, the UK and the US. Slovenia experienced a negative growth rate and other slow-growing countries included Japan and Germany; both experienced less than 1% average annual growth in real GDP.

To obtain a solution to our second problem, we have to specify a target level of output ($\bar{y}$) such that cumulative real GDP throughout the period is greater than the target: $\sum_{t=\tau}^{\tau+\Gamma} \left(CIX_o^t + G^t\right) \geq \bar{y}_o$. In our first simulation we assume that each country has a target for cumulative real GDP equal to its

---

[2]We calculate the average annual growth rate using the formula for the future value of an annuity flow: $FV = A \times \left(\frac{(1+r)^t}{r}\right)$, where FV equals cumulative real GDP for the seventeen year period, A = real GDP in 1995, and t = 17.

actual cumulative real GDP during 1995–2011. Given this country specific target, this problem chooses government purchases (G) to minimize the cumulative debt. The optimal time to begin production (τ) is again 1995, and as before production occurs over the entire time period. In addition to actual debt accumulated during the 1995–2011 period, Table 5.3 reports the simulated debt given the GDP growth target. Luxembourg would have experienced a surplus equal to 24.7% of 2011 real GDP, which was equal to the actual surplus. For the other countries the cumulative debt is smaller (or cumulative surplus is larger) when resources are optimally allocated across time. Greece, with the largest actual debt to GDP ratio, also had the largest simulated debt to GDP ratio, with both actual and simulated debt exceeding 100% of real GDP.

Chapter 6

Some Limitations of Two DEA Models

In this chapter we consider two DEA models, the first is the DEA specification with a non-Archimedean infinitesimal and the second is the 'super-efficiency' model. The first of these was introduced to address Charnes, Cooper and Rhodes' (1978) concern that the piecewise linear construction of technology in DEA may yield vertical and horizontal extensions, and the second was introduced by Andersen and Petersen (1993) to provide a means to 'break ties', i.e., to allow for ranking the DMU:s in a sample which are technically efficient.

For these two problems we provide an example which demonstrates the limitations of these 'fixes.' In the case of the non-Archimedian, we show that a slight change in the choice of the approximation for the non-Archimedean can result in changes in the rankings of DMUs. For the super-efficiency model we provide an example showing that this approach may fail to break ties.

6.1 The Non-Archimedean and DEA

(by Färe, R., Grosskopf, S. and Yaisawarng, S.)

A non-Archimedean, which, informally defined, is a positive number smaller than any positive real number (see Davis, 1976) was introduced in the original DEA model in Charnes, Cooper and Rhodes (1978) in order to assess efficiency relative to an input/output Pareto-Koopmans efficient

87

subset rather than relative to isoquants, which might have horizontal or vertical segments that are not Pareto-Koopmans efficient.[1]

Following Banker, Charnes and Cooper (1984),[2] the DEA score for DMU k may be computed using the so-called Multiplier Model by solving the following problem translated to the notation used here

$$\max \lambda = \sum_{m=1}^{M} p_m y_{k'm}$$

$$s.t. \quad \sum_{n=1}^{N} w_n x_{k'n} = 1$$

$$\sum_{m=1}^{M} p_m y_{km}$$

$$-\sum_{n=1}^{N} w_n x_{kn} \leqq 0, \quad k = 1, \ldots, K$$

$$p_m \geqq \epsilon, \quad w_n \geqq \epsilon, \quad m = 1, \ldots, M, \quad n = 1, \ldots, N$$

where ϵ is the non-Archimedean. x_{kn} and y_{km} are non-negative inputs and outputs.

The virtual multipliers (prices) w_n and p_m are bounded below by ϵ.

Färe and Hunsaker (1986) show that DEA models that involve a non-Archimedean may have efficiency scores that are not independent of the non-Archimedean quantity. Here we carry the analysis of the non-Archimdean in DEA one step further. We show that if it is taken to be a real number as in Lewin and Morey (1981), the relative rankings of DMU's may depend on the number chosen.

In any numerical estimation of an efficiency score in DEA, ϵ must be taken as a (small) real number. Here we show by example that the efficiency score is affected by that numerical choice of ϵ and also — perhaps more

---

[1] They were seeking an alternative to the *ad hoc* method proposed by Farrell (1957), which was to add points at infinity to the sample data. Interestingly, Farrell claims that doing so would provide horizontal and vertical extensions to the boundary of the isoquant.

[2] See also Cooper, Seiford and Zhu (2004).

importantly — that the *ranking* of the DMUs may change under different choices of ϵ.

Suppose that the DMUs and their corresponding input and output quantities are given below in Table 6.1:

Table 6.1. Data.

DMU	Input 1	Input 2	Output
1	1	1	1
2	1	2	1
3	1.000005	1.000005	1

For the relevant DMUs, the efficiency scores are displayed below in Table 6.2:

Table 6.2. Efficiency scores.

DMU	$\epsilon^{10^{-5}}$	$\epsilon^{10^{-6}}$
1	1.000000	1.000000
2	0.999990	0.999999
3	0.999995	0.999995

These results show that the efficiency score for DMU2 changes when ϵ changes from $\epsilon = 10^{-5}$ to $\epsilon = 10^{-6}$. The table also shows that DMU3 is more efficient than DMU2 if $\epsilon = 10^{-5}$, but the reverse holds when $\epsilon = 10^{-6}$.

The example introduced here demonstrates that the efficiency score and efficiency *ranking* depend on the choice of ϵ as well as the data when the DEA model includes a non-Archimedean. Thus not only is this method potentially inconsistent in ranking DMU efficiency, but it can also yield efficiency values which depend arbitrarily on a subjective choice of ϵ. Finally, comparing DMU1 above (the efficient observation) with DMU2 shows that the DEA method with the non-Archimedean is not alway sensitive to 'large' inefficiencies.

6.2 Super-Efficiency and Zeros

Von Neumann (1938, 1945) in his Activity Analysis (AA) model assumed that each input $x_{kn}, k = 1, \ldots, K$ (observations or DMU's, $n = 1, \ldots, N$

(types of inputs) and each output $y_{km}, k = 1, \ldots, K, m = 1, \ldots, M$ (types of outputs) are strictly positive. Charnes, Cooper and Rhodes (1978), made the same assumption for their DEA model.[3]

Kemeney, Morgenstern and Thompson (1956) generalized the von Neumann model by relaxing the strict positivity requirement. Their relaxed requirement was that each firm or DMU used some input to produce some output, and that each input and output is used and produced by some DMU, i.e., they were allowing for some zeros in the data. In Chapter 2 we have addressed these conditions.

When used to evaluate efficiency for samples of DMU's, both the AA and DEA models may have more than one 'efficient' unit, which suggests a lack of discriminatory power with respect to efficiency rankings. To address this problem, Andersen and Petersen (1993) introduced the notion of super-efficiency. This method evaluates each DMU relative to the sample excluding that DMU's data in the reference set.

It is well known that the super-efficiency model may yield infeasibilities, both in the case of constant and variable returns to scale.

In a recent paper Lee and Zhu (2012) note that '... none of the existing studies on super-efficiency infeasibility consider the situation when zero data exists.' Here we address super-efficiency in a VRS model with respect to:

(i) infeasibility
(ii) its power to discriminate among efficient DMU's.

We look at the two issues via examples which allow for zeros, but satisfy the conditions proposed by Kemeny, Morgenstern and Thompson (1956).

Assume that there are two DMU's $k = 1, 2$ which use a single input $x_k (N = 1)$ to produce two outputs $y_{km}, m = 1, 2$. The data is summarized in the table below.

DMU	1	2
x	1	1
y_1	1	0
y_2	0	1

---

[3]The reference technology of the Activity Analysis and DEA models are identical.

This example satisfies the Kemeny, Morgenstern and Thompson (1956) conditions: each firm uses some input to produce some output, and the input is used by at least one DMU (in this case both DMUs) and each output is produced by at least one DMU. Note that there are zeros in the data: here $y_{12} = y_{21} = 0$.

The output oriented DEA score for DMU1 is estimated as

$$\max \theta_1 \qquad (6.1)$$

$$s.t. \quad z_1 \cdot 1 + z_2 \cdot 1 \leqq 1$$

$$z_1 \cdot 1 + z_2 \cdot 0 \geqq 1 \cdot \theta_1$$

$$z_1 \cdot 0 + z_2 \cdot 1 \geqq 0 \cdot \theta_1$$

$$z_1, z_2 \geqq 0$$

$$z_1 + z_2 = 1$$

where z_1, z_2 are the intensity variables, summing to one to allow for variable returns to scale (VRS). DMU1 is efficient, i.e., $\theta_1^* = 1$, as is DMU2. Thus the two DMUs are equally ranked in the VRS model.

Now consider the 'super-efficiency' score λ, for DMU2:

$$\max \lambda_2 \qquad (6.2)$$

$$s.t. \quad z_1 \cdot 1 \leqq 1$$

$$z_1 \cdot 1 \geqq \lambda_2 \cdot 0$$

$$z_1 \cdot 0 \geqq \lambda_2 \cdot 1$$

$$z_1 \geqq 0$$

$$z_1 = 1.$$

The solution to this problem is $\lambda_2^* = 0$. The super-efficiency score for DMU1 is also zero, i.e., $\lambda_1^* = 0$, thus both DMUs have the same super-efficiency score. This demonstrates that the super-efficiency model does not necessarily discriminate among efficient DMUs.

References

Afriat, S.N. 1972, Efficiency estimation of production functions, *International Economic Review* 13:3, 568–598.

Anderson, P. and Petersen, N.C. 1993, A procedure for ranking efficient units in DEA, *Management Science* 39:10, 1261–1264.

Baldani, J., Bradfield, J. and Turner R. 1996, *Mathematical Economics*, Dryden Press, Orlander.

Banker, R.E., Charnes, A. and Cooper, W.W. 1984, Some models for estimating technical and scale inefficiencies in data envelopment analysis, *Management Science* 30:9, 1078–1092.

Banker, R.D. and Morey, R.C. 1986a, Efficiency analysis for exogenously fixed inputs and outputs, *Operations Research* 34:4, 513–521.

Banker, R.D. and Morey, R.C. 1986b, The use of categorical variables in data envelopment analysis, *Management Science* 32:12, 1613–1627.

Baumgärtner, S., Dykhoff, H., Faber, M. Proops, J. and Schiller, J. 2001, The concept of joint production and ecological economics, *Ecological Economics* 30, 365–372.

Berge, C. 1963, *Topological Spaces*, Oliver and Boyd, Edinburgh.

Bobzin, H. 1998, *Indivisibilities*, Physica, Heidelberg.

Byrnes, P., Färe, R. and Grosskopf, S. 1984, Measuring Productive Efficiency: An application to Illinois Strip Mines, *Management Science* 30:6, 671–681.

Caves, D., Christensen, L. and Diewert, W.D. 1982, The economic theory of index numbers and the measurement of input, output and productivity, *Econometrica* 50:6, 1393–1414.

Chambers, R.G., Chung, Y. and Färe, R. 1998, Profit, directional distance functions, and Nerlovian efficiency, *Journal of Optimization Theory and Applications* 98:2, 351–364.

Chambers, R.G. and Färe, R. 1994, Hicks neutrality and trade biased growth: A taxonomy, *Journal of Economic Theory* 64, 554–567.

94 *Färe, R., Grosskopf, S. and Margaritis, D.*

Charnes, A., Cooper, W.W. and Rhodes, E. 1978, Measuring the efficiency of decision making units, *European Journal of Operational Research* 2, 429–444.

Cooper, W.W., Seiford, L.M. and Zhu, J. 2004, *Handbook on Data Envelopment Analysis*, Springer, New York.

Davis, M. 1976, *Applied Nonstandard Analysis*, John Wiley & Sons.

Dorfman, R., Samuelson, P. and Solow, R.M. 1958, *Linear Programming and Economic Analysis*, Dover, New York.

Eichengreen, B. and Wyplosz, C. 1998, The stability pact: More than a mere nuisance?, *Economic Policy* 13:26, 65–113.

Färe, R. and Grosskopf, S. 2010a, Directional distance functions and slack-based measures of efficiency, *European Journal of Operational Research* 200, 320–322.

Färe, R. and Grosskopf, S. 2010b, Directional distance functions and slack-based measures of efficiency: Some clarifications, *European Journal of Operational Research* 206, 702.

Färe, R. and Grosskopf, S. 1996, *Intertemporal Production Frontiers: With Dynamic DEA*, Kluwer, Boston.

Färe, R. and Grosskopf, S. 2012, DEA, directional distance functions and positive affine data transformations, *Omega* 41, 28–30.

Färe, R. and Grosskopf, S. 2004, *New Directions: Efficiency and productivity*, Kluwer Academic Publishers, Boston.

Färe, R., Grosskopf, S. and Logan, J. 1983, The relative efficiency of Illinois public utilities, *Resources and Energy* 5, 349–367.

Färe, R., Grosskopf, S. and Margaritis, D. 2011, The diet problem and DEA, *Journal of the Operational Research Society* 62:7, 1420–1422.

Färe, R., Grosskopf, S. and Margaritis, D. 2010, Time substitution with application to Data Envelopment Analysis, *European Journal of Operational Research* 206:3, 686–690.

Färe, R., Grosskopf, S. and Margaritis, D. 2012, Pricing Decision-Making Units, *Journal of the Operational Research Society* 64, 619–621.

Färe, R., Grosskopf, S., Margaritis, D. and Weber, W. 2012, Technological change and timing reduction in greenhouse gas emissions, *Journal of Productivity Analysis* 37, 205–216.

Färe, R., Grosskopf, S. and Whittaker, G. 2013, Directional distance functions: Endogenous directions based on exogenous normalization constraints, *Journal of Productivity Analysis* 40:3, 267–269.

Färe, R. and Hunsaker, W. 1986, Notions of efficiency ad their reference sets, *Management Science* 237–243.

Färe, R. and Lovell, C.A.K. 1978, Measuring the technical efficiency of production, *Journal of Economic Theory* 19, 150–162.

Färe, R. and Primont, D. 1995, *Multi-Output production and duality: Theory and applications*, Kluwer Academic Publishers, Boston.

Farrell, M.J. 1957, The measurement of productive efficiency, *The Journal of the Royal Statistical Society*, Series A, General 120, part 3, 253–281.

Gale, D. 1960, *Theory of Linear Models*, University of Chicago Press, Chicago.

Kemeny, J.G., Morgenstern, O. and Thompson, G.L. 1956, A generalization of the von Neumann model of expanding economy, *Econometrica* 24, 115–135.

Koopmans, C. 1951, *Activity Analysis of Production and Allocation*, John Wiley and Sons, New York.

Kuosmanen, T. 2005, Weak disposability in nonparametric analysis with undesirable outputs, *American Journal of Agricultural Economics* 87:4, 1077–1082.

Lewin, A. and Morey, R.C. 1981, Measuring the relative efficiency and output potential of public sector organizations, *International Journal of Policy Analysis and Information Systems* 5, 267–285.

Lee, H.-S. and Zhu, J. 2012, Super-efficiency infeasibilities and zeros in DEA, *European Journal of Operational Research* 216, 429–433.

Luenberger, D.G., 1992, Benefit functions and duality, *Journal of Mathematical Economics* 21, 461–481.

Luenberger, D.G., 1995, *Microeconomic Theory*, McGraw Hill, New York.

Magill, M. and Quinzii, M. 1996, *Theory of Incomplete Markets*, MIT Press, Cambridge.

von Neumann, J. (1937, 1945), Über ein ökonomisches gleichungssystem und eine verallgemeinerung des Brouwerschen Fixpunktsatzes, in K. Menger, ed., *Ergebnisses eines Mathematischen Kolloquiums*, reprinted as A model of general economic equilibrium, *Review of Economic Studies* 13:1, 1–9.

von Neumann, J. and Morgenstern, O. 1944, *Theory of Games and Economic Behavior*, Princeton University Press, Princeton.

Schuknecht, L. 2002, The implementation of the stability and growth pact, *OECD Journal on Budgeting*, 81–116.

Schuknecht, L., Moutot, P., Rother, P. and Stark, J. 2011, The stability and growth pact: Crisis and reform. European Central Bank, Occasional paper Series, no. 1209.

Shephard, R.W. 1953, *Cost and Production Functions*, Princeton University Press, Princeton.

Shephard, R.W. 1970, *Theory of Cost and Production Functions*, Princeton University Press, Princeton.

Shephard, R.W. 1974, *Indirect Production Functions*, Anton Hain, Cambridge, MA.

Shephard, R.W. and Färe, R. 1974, The law of diminishing returns, Zeitschrift für Nationalökonomie 34, 69–90.

Shephard, R.W. and Färe, R. 1980, *Dynamic Theory of Production Correspondences*, Anton Hain, Cambridge, MA.

Tone, K. 2001, A slack-based measure of efficiency in data envelopment analysis, *European Journal of Operational Research* 130, 498–509.

Wyplosz, C. 2012, *Fiscal rules: Theoretical issues and historical experiences*, The Graduate Institute, Geneva.

Index

Printed in the United States
By Bookmasters